Potatoes:
Mashed and More

Potatoes:
Mashed and More

First published in 2000
by Hamlyn
a division of Octopus Publishing Group Limited
2–4 Heron Quays, London E14 4JP

Distributed in the United States and Canada by
Sterling Publishing Co., Inc.
387 Park Avenue South, New York, NY 10016–8810

ISBN 0 600 60405 5

Printed in Hong Kong

Cover photography and Special photography: Philip Webb
All other photography: Octopus Publishing Group Limited
Home Economist: Dagmar Vesely

NOTES

1 The American Egg Board advises that eggs should not be consumed raw. This book contains some dishes made with raw or lightly cooked eggs. It is prudent for more vulnerable people such as pregnant and nursing mothers, invalids, the elderly, babies and young children to avoid uncooked or lightly cooked dishes made with eggs.

2 Meat and poultry should be cooked thoroughly. To test if poultry is cooked, pierce the flesh through the thickest part with a skewer or fork – the juices should run clear, never pink or red. Keep refrigerated until ready for cooking.

3 This book includes dishes made with nuts and nut derivatives. It is advisable for those with known allergic reactions to nuts and nut derivatives and those who may be potentially vulnerable to these allergies, such as pregnant and nursing mothers, invalids, the elderly, babies, and children, to avoid dishes made with nuts and nut oils. It is also prudent to check the labels of prepepared ingredients for the possible inclusion of nut derivatives.

Contents

Introduction

The potato is a starchy edible tuber, which grows at the end of underground stems of the plant, *Solanum tuberosum*, a member of the nightshade family. Above ground, the plant has a stem and coarse, dark green leaves resembling those of the tomato. Its flowers range from white to purple. The tuber has external buds, or "eyes", which can sprout into new plants.

Few foods have a more legendary past, natural diversity, fascination for scientists or greater potential to feed the world's population than the potato. It is the most familiar of all vegetables and one of the world's most important food crops. There are now more varieties than ever before, adapted for different climatic zones and grown in about 130 countries around the world. The potato can be cooked in more ways than any other vegetable. It is easy to grow, inexpensive to buy, and extremely filling.

Potato history

Potatoes are native to South America. The first archaeological evidence dates back almost 6,000 years to areas in the Peruvian Andes where the potato plant is part of the native flora. It was cultivated in Peru and Bolivia and was a staple of the Inca diet. The influence of potatoes permeated the Incan culture and potato-shaped pottery complete with "eyes" is commonly found at excavated sites.

Incan units of time correlated to how long it took for a potato to cook to various consistencies; potatoes were even used to divine the truth and predict weather.

The potato was introduced to Europe from South America by Spanish explorers towards the end of the 16th century. Cultivation spread slowly from Spain to Italy, then Belgium, Germany, and Switzerland. It took a very long time for the crop to become established in some countries. In Germany, for example, potatoes were widely cultivated only after the cereal crops failed in 1743 and 1755. In France the general populace had to be tricked into growing and eating them. In 1785 King Louis XVI had a field of potatoes planted near Paris and had a guard posted around it during the day. The local peasants were convinced that the crop must be very valuable, so they stole the plants at night and planted them in their own fields. And although the potato was brought to England in the 17th century, it was not until the 19th century that farmers in England and Scotland actually started to cultivate it on a large scale.The story in Ireland was quite different, however. There the potato was widely grown by the beginning of the 17th century. It was early 18th-century Irish immigrants who brought the potato to the United States, since it had failed to spread here directly from

South America. The first large scale cultivation of the potato in the United States was in New Hampshire.

By the middle of the 19th century the potato had become the staple diet in Ireland and was also relied on as animal fodder. This dependence on potatoes led to intensive cultivation, and the dominance of one prolific variety of potato, which created the ripe circumstances for the rapid spread of the fungal disease, blight. The potato blight struck Ireland three times in the 1840s, each time destroying most of the crop. The country's virtual monoculture meant that there was little else for the people or their livestock to eat. Relief efforts were mounted but they were only partially effective, and over a million people died. Between 1841 and 1851 Ireland's population fell dramatically from 8.2 million to 6.6 million as a result of starvation, disease, and emigration — to England and especially to the United States. Nearly 200 years later, during World War II, it was the potato that helped to save people in Europe from starvation.

The second half of the 20th century saw the introduction of and increasing reliance on convenience foods. There is now a large worldwide market for an extensive range of dehydrated and frozen potato products, the most important of which is

undoubtedly the French fry. This was first encountered by American soldiers in Belgium during World War I.

Today scientists and agriculturists continue to study and develop new potato varieties. This results in making them higher yielding, more disease resistant and suited to a variety of climates worldwide. In developing countries the production of potatoes is increasing faster than that of any other crop.

Folklore

It is interesting to examine the different ways in which the potato has been regarded over time. While the Incas worshiped potato gods, the vegetable was often feared, reviled, and shunned for the first few centuries following its arrival in Europe. At various times it was blamed for leprosy, scrofula, and flatulence, and was considered poisonous, since it came from the same family as deadly nightshade. It was also, however, attributed with the ability to cure impotence, and had a reputation as an aphrodisiac in Shakespeare's England, according to *The Merry Wives of Windsor*.

Other sayings and superstitions relating to potatoes are of unknown origin. Laying a potato peeling at the door of a girl on May Day was said to show her that you disliked her, while a woman expecting a baby was not to eat potatoes, especially at night, or her baby would be born with a big head. A potato carried in the pocket was believed to cure rheumatism and eczema. Similarly, carrying a peeled potato in a pocket on the same side as a bad tooth would cure the tooth as soon as the potato fell apart. A person with a wart was advised to rub it with a cut potato, then bury the potato in the ground. As the potato rotted in the ground, the belief was that the wart would disappear.

Nutrition and health

With its high starch content, the potato was long regarded as being a "fattening" food, but now a more complete understanding of nutrition has led to its rehabilitation. The addition of too much fat when cooking and serving potatoes is now recognized as being the culprit. By itself, the potato is in fact a near perfect food. It is 99.9% fat free and yet it is rich in nutrients, containing a number of minerals and vitamins that are important for a healthy and nutritious diet.

According to food experts, a diet of potatoes and milk will supply all the nutrients the human body needs. Although potatoes are about 80% water, they provide a valuable source of easily digested starch, vitamin C, protein, potassium, iron, thiamine, niacin, and dietary fiber, while containing almost no fat or cholesterol.

The vitamin C content is highest in freshly harvested potatoes — particularly "new" ones — and steadily decreases thereafter. After three months' storage, the vitamin C content is less than half the original. Lengthy soaking of potatoes in cold water also diminishes their vitamin C content and should be

---

Nutritional composition of a potato

Water	81%
Starch	16%
Minerals and trace elements	1%
Vitamins	0.7%
Fiber	0.6%
Protein	0.35%
Sugar	0.27%
Fat	0.08%

Nutritional values per 100 g (3½ oz) raw potato

Energy	79 kcal
Protein	2.1 g
Carbohydrate	17.2 g
Fat	0.2 g
Fiber	1.3 g
Sodium	trace

Introduction

avoided. Many of the vitamins and minerals found in potatoes are concentrated in or just under the skin and are therefore best retained by cooking potatoes in their skin or by peeling them as lightly as possible. Potato skins are also high in fiber. Concerns over agricultural chemical residues in skins, which are not removed by scrubbing potatoes with water, can be addressed by eating organically grown potatoes.

Potato varieties

Potatoes vary considerably in size and may be round, oval, long, or kidney shaped, depending on variety. Small long potatoes are called "fingers" or "fingerlings." Potatoes may be red–or brown–skinned or, more rarely, blue, black, or purple. The flesh is mostly in the white to yellow color range, although there are also varieties with pink, red, and purple-streaked flesh.

Cataloging the endless varieties of potatoes is difficult. Popular varieties change rapidly, coming into favor with growers because they keep well or are resistant to disease, only to be ousted by newer, even hardier varieties with higher yields.

The flavor of a potato depends on both its variety and its inherent texture. How and where it is grown and in what soil, and the weather in any one season can all affect its ultimate flavor and quality. This explains why the same variety of potato may taste better, or have a slightly different flavor at some times than others.

"New" and "old"

In most countries potatoes are defined as "new" or "old," and they are distinguished by texture as being mealy or waxy. Here potatoes are also commonly classified by shape, skin color, and use.

Although in some countries new potatoes are specific varieties, here new potatoes are simply young potatoes of any variety that are harvested before they have completely converted their sugar content into starch and while the skin is still so wispy that you can easily rub it off with your fingers. They have a crisp waxy texture and are known for their delicate and sweet flavor. They are best cooked by boiling or steaming them in their skins and they taste great in potato salads. New potatoes can also be roasted.

"Old" potatoes can also be any variety and are simply those potatoes that are left until they are fully matured. The different varieties are then divided by use into bakers, boilers, and all-purpose potatoes.

Waxy versus mealy potatoes

Potatoes with a firm, waxy texture have a high moisture content, low starch, and thin skins. They do not break up during cooking and are therefore ideal for boiling and sautéing, for use in salads, and for any dish where the potatoes need to remain intact after being sliced thinly and then baked, for example a gratin. Waxy potatoes become glutinous when they are overprocessed and are therefore not recommended for mashing. Mealy-textured potatoes contain more starch than waxy potates and they tend to break up more easily once they are cooked. They are generally best used for mashing, roasting, and baking in their skins. Both waxy and mealy varieties of potatoes can be used to make French fries.

Although undoubtedly some potato varieties are much better for baking than for boiling and vice versa, if you do want baked potatoes and you have only waxy ones in the house, then you can still use them for baking. You will simply get a different-textured potato. In fact, the majority of potato varieties are neither especially mealy nor especially waxy; most potato varieties can be boiled, roasted, baked, sautéed, fried and mashed. There are also a number of all-purpose potato varieties, which have a moderate moisture and starch content as well as a firm texture. They

Introduction

can be used for almost anything — except perhaps in potato salads. They don't disintegrate when they are cooked, but they don't always have the best flavor.

Sweet potato

The sweet potato, *Ipomoea batatas*, is the starchy tuberous root of a tropical vine and despite its name, it is not actually related to the potato. However, it can be prepared and cooked in exactly the same ways as potatoes, and is most successful when it is baked and served with butter or simply mashed and served as an accompaniment to a meal. Sweet potatoes are sometimes wrongly referred to as yams, which are in fact another species of tuber.

Sweet potatoes are generally elongated and knobbly, with pink skin and white, yellow, or orange flesh. The yellowish flesh indicates the presence of carotene, which is a source of vitamin A. Always choose small or medium-sized sweet potatoes, that are firm and well shaped; avoid any with cracks. There are some differences in flavor between varieties of sweet pototo which result from the balance of sugar and starch. Sweet potatoes do not store very well, so it is best to eat them as soon as possible after purchase, but they are cultivated year round and are readily available in supermarkets.

Popular potato varieties

BAKERS

Lemhi Russey
Purple Peruvian (finger)
Russet Burbank or Idaho

BOILERS

All Red
Anoka
Blossom
Huckleberry
Rose Finn Apple (finger)
Ruby Crescent (finger)

ALL-PURPOSE

All Blue
Bintje
Desiree
German Butterball
Long White
Red Gold
White Rose
Yellow Finn
Yukon Gold

Choosing and storing potatoes

When buying potatoes, choose ones that are well formed, with firm smooth skins. They should smell fresh. Avoid any with discoloration, cracks, bruises, or soft spots. Don't buy or use potatoes with a greenish tinge to the skins — these have been badly stored, exposed to light, and are unfit for eating.

New potatoes should be small and fresh: Ragged skins that can be pulled off easily show that the potatoes are very fresh. Buy new potatoes in small quantities only and use them quickly, as they do not keep very well and they lose their flavor and texture after just a couple of days. Allow 6–8 oz of potatoes per person.

Keep potatoes in a cool, dark, well-ventilated place. In these conditions old potatoes can be safely stored for several months at a temperature of 45–50°F. Buy only a week's supply at a time if you must store them at higher temperatures, since heat causes them to sprout and shrivel. Do not store potatoes in the refrigerator. Below about 40°F, potato starch turns to sugar and results in the darkening of potatoes during cooking. Although unattractive, this is not harmful; the dark spots simply reveal the presence of a higher concentration of sugars. The process can be reversed by keeping the potatoes at room temperature, but still stored in the dark, for a couple of days.

Do not wash potatoes before storing, as washing speeds decay. Brown paper bags are best for storing small quantities of potatoes. If you buy potatoes in a plastic bag, tear the bag so that the potatoes don't sweat. It is particularly important that the storage place is dark in order to prevent the development of solanine, which causes potatoes to turn green. Although the green coloring (chlorophyll) itself is harmless, the green parts also contain high levels of poisonous alkaloids and should never be eaten. Make sure all the green parts of the potato are cut away; the rest will then be alright to eat. Never use potatoes where more than one tenth of the skin has turned green.

Potato sprouts also contain high levels of these poisonous alkaloids and should never be eaten. Similarly, once these sprouting parts are cut away, a sprouted potato is safe to eat, although it becomes softer and deteriorates in flavor and nutritional content.

Cooking methods

Potatoes can be cooked in a multitude of ways, and used whole, grated, sliced, or chopped. They form the basis of many traditional and regional dishes the world over, for example Swiss rôsti, Irish

Cooking Methods

colcannon, French gratin dauphinoise and Niçoise salad, the Spanish omelet, and Italian gnocchi. You can boil or steam them and serve them as they are, or mash them with butter and milk or with additional ingredients. Bake them in their skins, roast or sauté them, serve them as fries, barbecue or grill them — the options are endless. Other than its obvious form as a vegetable in soups, main courses, and side dishes, the potato can be mixed with flour to make pastry, bread, and biscuits, and is used in sauces and some dessert recipes.

The widespread use of the potato accounts for the numerous culinary utensils that have been developed especially for it. Consider the potato peeler, the special knives available for cutting regular slices and potato straws, the French fry cutter, the potato ricer, the mashed potato scoop and the potato masher among others.

Boiling and steaming

Potatoes cooked in their skins are better for you and tastier, too. Leaving potatoes unpeeled retains much of the nutrients and flavor found near the skin and affords the potato flesh some protection from the cooking water or steam, which dissolves the nutrients. If you must peel potatoes before cooking, use a vegetable parer rather than a knife so as to pare the skin as thinly as possible.

Whether you keep the skins on after cooking is often a matter of personal choice.

Potatoes should spend as little time as possible in water because of its detrimental effect on nutrients. Cooking potatoes using the least amount necessary of boiling water, rather than bringing them to a boil from cold will reduce their contact time with water.

However, opinions differ as to which of these methods you should use. Whether you prefer to cook potatoes using cold water or add them to a saucepan of boiling water, use equally sized whole potatoes or cut the potatoes into even-sized pieces so that they will cook evenly. Cover the pot, again to reduce cooking time and therefore time spent in water, and cook the potatoes until tender–10–15 minutes for new potatoes and about 20 minutes for old ones, although it does depend on their size. Reduce the heat to cook the potatoes gently, since fast boiling causes them to bump against each other and break up. While this is not so important if you are intending to make mashed potatoes, it is not desirable for gratins or potato salads. When just tender, drain the potatoes thoroughly and return them to the pot. Allow them to steam for a minute or so, or alternatively leave them in the pot covered with a clean dish towel to

absorb the steam and produce dry rather than sodden potatoes.

If you are peeling potatoes, ideally do so just before cooking. However, if this is not feasible, place the peeled potatoes in a bowl of water to prevent them from drying out and, in the case of some varieties, from discoloring on exposure to air. Do not soak them too long, however, as vitamins will be lost in the process.

Old potatoes are prone to blackening after cooking. This can easily be prevented by adding a good squeeze of lemon juice or a teaspoon of vinegar to the cooking water.

In terms of retaining nutrients and flavor, steaming is a better method for cooking potatoes than boiling, although it takes a little longer.

To peel hot potatoes after boiling or steaming them, hold them in a dish towel and remove the skins using a potato peeler. However, this can be a painful and tedious process, and it is not recommended if you are preparing potatoes for more than three people.

Serve boiled or steamed potatoes, with or without their skins, plain or jazzed up with a pat of butter or a tasty pesto to accompany them.

Cooking Methods

Mashed Potatoes

There are various ways of making mashed potatoes but the basic principles are the same. Cut the potatoes into similarly sized pieces so that they cook evenly, then boil or steam them as above. Drain thoroughly. Peel the potatoes if they were cooked in their skins, then mash them until they are really smooth. If the basic mashed potatoes are too watery, dry them off in the pot before proceeding. Add butter and warm, not cold, milk then beat until light and fluffy. Season with salt and pepper and serve.

The character of mashed potatoes depends on the texture of the potatoes used. Any variety of potato can be used. Mealy potato varieties produce a fluffier mashed potato, while waxy potatoes produce a denser, richer version, that is inclined to become gluey.

Mashed potatoes can be stiff or soft; they can be mashed using a potato masher or a fork, or whipped until light with a hand whisk. Processing it in a blender or food processor will produce a purée — runnier than mashed potatoes, and smooth like a cream sauce. Mashed potatoes or purée can also be made by passing cooked potatoes through a food mill or a potato ricer. While traditional mashed potatoes are smooth and fluffy, made with butter and milk, modern mashed potatoes may be made with olive oil. Serve mashed potatoes just as they are or pile it into a shallow heatproof dish, fork up the top and brown it in the broiler. Mashed potatoes reheat well but do not freeze. Leftover mashed potatoes can, however, be used as the basis for other recipes, for example in potato pastry, fish cakes, or for bread making.

Baking

Baking retains all the goodness and flavor of potatoes. Although any variety can be baked, the best potatoes for baking are mealy varieties. The potato becomes fluffy inside as its starch expands under the intense heat.

Scrub potatoes for baking, then pat them dry. Carefully cut away any damaged parts and prick the skins in a couple of places with a fork or a sharp knife. This allows steam to escape during cooking and prevents the potatoes from exploding or bursting apart in the oven. To produce very crisp skins, brush the potatoes with oil and sprinkle them with salt. If you prefer a soft skin, wrap each potato in a square of kitchen foil.

Place the potatoes directly on an oven shelf and bake them at 400°F, for about 1–1½ hours, depending on their size, until they are tender. To check if the potatoes are cooked through, squeeze them gently — they should feel soft to the touch — alternatively pierce them with a skewer or sharp knife.

If you are short of time for cooking the potatoes, cut them in half lengthwise and brush the cut surfaces with olive oil. This will reduce the cooking time by up to half. Using a potato baker, which has metal prongs to spear through the potatoes and conduct the heat more quickly, will also reduce the cooking time. Simply pushing a metal skewer through each potato before baking has the same effect.

Potatoes can also be "baked" using a microwave oven. Wash, dry, and prick the potatoes as usual and wrap each one in a paper towel. Cook on "high" for about 5–6 minutes for one potato, 10–12 minutes for two potatoes, or 18–20 minutes for four. Microwaving produces a cooked potato with a soft skin, which is quite different from a conventionally baked potato, but tastes good and is great when time is a consideration.

Serve baked potatoes straight from the oven, simply split open and smothered with butter, or with other fillings added to the potato. Alternatively, scoop out the potato flesh, mix it with other ingredients such as tapenade or a soft creamy cheese and pile it back into the skins.

Cooking Methods

To bake new potatoes, cut them in half and place them on a large piece of buttered foil. Sprinkle them with salt and pepper, seal the foil, and place on a baking sheet. Bake in a preheated oven, 350°F, for about 1 hour.

Roasting

A perfect roast potato should never be greasy. It should be dry and crisp on the outside and soft and fluffy inside. The desired crunchy and uneven, rather than smooth, surface of roast potatoes is achieved by parboiling the potatoes first, then roughing up their exteriors with a fork or shaking them in a colander. Roast potatoes should not sit around after cooking, but are best eaten straight from the oven, while still piping hot and before they lose their crunchiness.

Use any variety of potato for roasting — a mealy one produces a fluffy inside, a waxy potato gives a soft smooth inside. Parboil the potatoes for 5 minutes first, then drain them thoroughly. Return them to the dry saucepan and lightly shake them against the sides of the pan to roughen the exteriors or score them with a fork. Allow to cool. Heat a little oil in a shallow ovenproof dish or a roasting pan, then add the parboiled roughened potatoes and turn them in the sizzling oil to coat them well. Roast at 375°F, for 45–60 minutes, basting the potatoes regularly and turning them once or twice.

The traditional way to roast potatoes is to place them around the meat, but roasting them in a separate shallow dish avoids contact with juices from the meat which makes the potatoes soggy. Add some herbs such as rosemary and some garlic to add flavor to the roasting potatoes, if liked. Another option is to roast the potatoes in oil for 30 minutes as above, then pour off any visible fat from the dish and continue cooking them by dry-roasting them for another 15 minutes or so, until cooked through and golden brown and crunchy on the outside. Serve immediately, sprinkled with salt.

Deep-frying

To make fries, peel potatoes and cut them into thick slices, then into sticks. Leave the potatoes in a bowl of cold water for 30 minutes to remove excess starch, otherwise they will stick together when fried. Drain the potatoes and pat dry well, using a dish towel or paper towels. It is important to dry the potatoes well, or the hot fat will foam up over the wet potatoes and can easily bubble over. Using a deep-fat fryer, heat the oil to 375°F, or until a fry dropped in rises to the surface immediately, surrounded by bubbles. Quarter-fill the frying basket with potatoes, lower it into the oil, and cook for 6–7 minutes, until the fries are soft but not browned. Raise the basket to drain the fries; repeat with

the rest of the potatoes. Fry all the fries for a second time, for 3 minutes, until golden and crisp. Drain and serve the fries immediately.

Game fries are peeled potatoes cut into wafer-thin slices, then deep-fried until golden and drained on paper towels.

Sautéing

Use a firm, waxy variety of potato for sautéing. Parboil the potatoes for about 10 minutes, until they are barely tender. Drain thoroughly, peel, and cut the potatoes into large even-sized chunks. Heat unsalted or clarified butter and oil together in a wide shallow heavy-based skillet until it is hot and foaming. Add the potatoes and sauté them gently until they are golden and crisp on all sides. Drain them on paper towels, sprinkle with salt, and serve them immediately.

Gratins

Served in the dish in which it is cooked, a good gratin is made by layering waxy potatoes with cream in a shallow ovenproof dish and then baking them slowly in the oven. The potato slices on the top become crisp and golden, hiding a rich creamy center beneath. The use of a shallow dish helps to ensure that every serving of the gratin receives some of the crusty topping, as well as some of the creamy center. The topping may be enhanced by a sprinkling of bread crumbs or some freshly grated cheese, such as Gruyère or Parmesan.

Indoor grilling

Grilling is possible for both new and sweet potatoes, and its characteristic scorch marks and smoky flavor gives them the look and taste of food cooked over an outdoor barbecue. Slices of peeled sweet potatoes will take 8–10 minutes each side to cook on a ridged grill pan. Grill small new potatoes, halved lengthwise, for 10 minutes each side.

Barbecueing

A barbecue can be unreliable for baking potatoes in their skins, as it is hard to estimate the temperature, so it is always best to bake them conventionally in an oven first for about 30 minutes (see page 17), then wrap them in foil, and place them in the hot ashes around the edges of the campfire or barbecue to finish cooking them.

To barbecue new potatoes, first boil them in their skins until they are just cooked. Carefully thread them onto skewers (presoaked if wooden, to prevent them from burning), brush with oil, and season them with salt and pepper. Place the skewered potatoes on the barbecue and cook for about 5–10 minutes, until the skins are crisp, turning them frequently during cooking.

Basic Techniques and Recipes

Chargrilled Rock Cornish Hen

A chargrilled Rock Cornish Hen looks impressive and cooks quickly, making it great for barbecues. This relatively simple job can be done at home. As well as the usual sharp knife, you will need one pair of long skewers per bird. If using wooden skewers, soak them in water for 30 minutes before use to prevent them from burning during cooking.

1. Put the hen, breast-side down, on a chopping board, Cut along each side of the backbone (poultry shears are ideal for this) and discard it.

2. Open out the bird and cut the wishbone in half. Turn the bird over so that it is breast-side up on the board and push down on it hard with the heel of your hand to break the breastbone and flatten it.

3. Trim off the ends of the wings. Cut a slit in the skin between the breastbone and each leg and tuck the ends of the legs into the slit.

4. To keep the bird flat as it cooks, thread the wooden skewers across the bird through both wings and legs. Wipe the bird with paper towels.

Harissa

Harissa is a fiery red, spicy hot chile paste, made from red peppers, chiles, garlic, and spices and is often used in North African cooking.

2 red bell peppers, roasted and skinned

1 oz fresh red chiles, chopped, seeds retained

1–2 garlic cloves, crushed

½ teaspoon coriander seeds, toasted

2 teaspoons caraway seeds

olive oil

salt

1. Put the red peppers, the chiles and their seeds, garlic, coriander, caraway seeds, and a pinch of salt in a food processor or blender, and mix, adding enough oil to make a thick paste.
2. Pack the harissa into a small, clean, dry jar and pour a layer of oil over the top. Cover with a tight-fitting lid and keep in the refrigerator.

Makes approx. 9 fl oz / Preparation time: 10 minutes

Aïoli

2 egg yolks

2–8 garlic cloves, crushed

½ teaspoon sea salt

1 tablespoon white wine vinegar

1¼ cups olive oil

pepper

1. Combine all the ingredients except the oil in a blender or food processor, season with pepper, and process briefly until pale and creamy.
2. With the motor running, gradually pour in the oil through the funnel until the mixture is thick, glossy, and pale. You may need to add a little boiling water to the mixture if it becomes too thick.
3. Transfer the mixture to a bowl. Taste, and adjust the seasoning if necessary, Cover with plastic wrap and refrigerate until required. The aïoli will keep for up to 3 days.

1 Soups

Serves 4 / Preparation time: 15 minutes / Cooking time: 20 minutes

Potato Soup with Parsley

6½ cups beef stock

4 potatoes, peeled and shredded

1 egg yolk

1 hard-cooked egg yolk, mashed

¼ cup light cream

½ cup freshly grated Parmesan cheese

1 tablespoon finely chopped parsley

salt and pepper

croûtons, to serve (see Tip)

1. Place the beef stock in a large saucepan and bring to a boil. Sprinkle the potatoes with salt and pepper, then drop them into the boiling stock. Cook for about 15 minutes, stirring occasionally.
2. Place the egg yolk in a soup tureen, beat well, then add the mashed hard-cooked egg yolk. Whisk the cream, Parmesan, and parsley into the egg mixture to blend.
3. Carefully pour about 1 cup of the stock into the egg mixture. Reheat the remaining stock and potatoes and gradually add them to the soup tureen. Sprinkle with croûtons and serve warm.

TIP To make croûtons, remove the crusts from 3 slices of bread. Using 1½ tablespoons of lemon juice, brush both sides of the bread slices with lemon juice. Toast the bread until pale brown on both sides. Cut into cubes and serve.

Chilled Potato Chowder

5 potatoes, peeled and diced

3 onions, sliced

1 can condensed cream of mushroom soup

2 tablespoons butter or margarine

1 quart milk

1 teaspoon prepared English mustard

salt and pepper

To garnish:

2 tablespoons cottage cheese

snipped chives

paprika

1. Place the potatoes and onions in a large saucepan. Add just enough water to cover, and cook the vegetables until tender. Drain the vegetables, then rub them through a coarse sieve into a clean saucepan.

2. Add the mushroom soup, butter or margarine, milk, mustard, and salt and pepper to taste. Stir well. Heat gently until the soup begins to simmer. Pour the soup into a bowl and leave to cool.

3. Cover the bowl and place the chowder in the refrigerator for at least 3 hours.

4. Serve the soup in chilled bowls, garnishing each serving with a little cottage cheese, a few snipped chives, and a light dusting of paprika.

Serves 4–6 / Preparation time: 15 minutes / Cooking time: about 30 minutes

Curried Apple and Potato Soup

¼ cup butter or margarine

1 small onion, chopped

2 dessert apples, such as Jonathan, peeled, cored, and sliced

1 tablespoon medium hot curry powder

2½ cups vegetable stock

10 oz potatoes, peeled and sliced

1¼ cups hot milk

salt

To garnish:

1 tablespoon butter

2–3 apple quarters, thinly sliced

cayenne pepper

1. Melt the butter or margarine in a saucepan and cook the chopped onion, stirring frequently, for 4–5 minutes, or until softened. Add the apples and curry powder and cook for a further 2 minutes, stirring.
2. Pour in the vegetable stock, then add the potatoes. Bring the mixture to a boil, lower the heat, and simmer for 15–18 minutes, or until the apples and potatoes are very soft.
3. Using a blender or food processor, purée the mixture, in batches until very smooth, and transfer to a clean saucepan. Reheat the purée and stir in the hot milk. Taste, and adjust the seasoning if necessary.
4. While the soup is reheating, melt the butter for the garnish in a small skillet, add the sliced apple, and sauté until crisp.
5. Serve the soup in warmed bowls, garnishing each serving with the sautéed apple and a light sprinkling of cayenne pepper.

Gruyère Soup with Bacon and Potatoes

2 tablespoons olive oil

3 slices of bacon, chopped

2 onions, finely chopped

2½ cups chicken stock

1 quart water

1¼ lb potatoes, peeled and cut into ½-inch cubes

¼ cup all-purpose flour

½ cup shredded Gruyère cheese

1 tablespoon medium dry sherry

1 teaspoon Worcestershire sauce

3 tablespoons finely chopped parsley

pepper

1. Heat the oil in a saucepan and cook the bacon and onions over a moderate heat until the onion is pale golden. Add the chicken stock, 2½ cups of the water, and the potatoes. Bring the mixture to a boil, then lower the heat, cover the pot, and simmer for 15 minutes, or until the potatoes are tender.
2. In a small bowl whisk the flour with the remaining water, then stir it into the soup. Cook, covered, for 5 minutes, stirring frequently.
3. In a blender or food processor, blend the Gruyère with 1¼ cups of the soup. Stir this purée back into the rest of the soup, then add the sherry and the Worcestershire sauce, with pepper, to taste. Simmer for 3–5 minutes.
4. Serve immediately, or cool, cover, and place in the refrigerator for up to 3 days. Heat thoroughly before serving, stirring in the parsley at the last moment.

Shrimp Vichyssoise

This sophisticated iced soup is made from some very humble ingredients—leeks and potatoes. It can be prepared 24 hours in advance and must be velvety smooth and well chilled.

2 lb leeks, trimmed and cleaned

¼ cup butter or margarine

1 onion, chopped

4½ cups chicken or vegetable stock

pinch of ground nutmeg

1½ lb baking potatoes, peeled and cubed

2½ cups milk

1¼ cups light cream

1 cup cooked peeled shrimp

⅔ cup heavy cream, chilled

salt and pepper

2 tablespoons snipped chives, to garnish

1. Slice off the green tops of the leeks and reserve for use in another recipe. Slice the white parts of the leeks thinly.

2. Melt the butter or margarine in a large saucepan. Add the leeks and onion and cook over a moderate heat for 5 minutes, stirring constantly. Do not allow the vegetables to change color.

3. Add the stock, nutmeg, and potatoes, with salt and pepper to taste. Bring the mixture to a boil, lower the heat, and cook, partially covered, for 25 minutes. Pour in the milk and simmer for a further 5–8 minutes. Cool slightly.

4. Using a blender or food processor, purée the mixture, in batches, until smooth, then rub it through a sieve into a bowl. Add the light cream and stir well. Cover the bowl and chill in the refrigerator for at least 3 hours. Just before serving, stir in the shrimp, swirl in the heavy cream, and add more salt and pepper if required.

5. Serve the soup in chilled bowls, garnishing each serving with a generous sprinkling of snipped chives.

FOOD FACT Vichyssoise was originally a chilled potato and leek cream soup created in the early 20th century by a French chef, who came from near Vichy in France. The name "vichyssoise" is often now given to any cold vegetable soup based on potatoes.

Serves 8 / Preparation time: 20 minutes / Cooking time: 55 minutes

Potato and Bacon Soup

1. Roughly chop the bacon slices.
2. Heat the oil in a large saucepan, add the chopped bacon, onion, and garlic and cook over a medium heat, stirring frequently, for 8–10 minutes, or until the onion is light brown and the bacon fairly crisp.
3. Add the stock, water, potatoes, leeks, marjoram, nutmeg, and Worcestershire sauce to the pot, with pepper to taste. Bring the mixture to a boil, lower the heat, cover, and simmer for 25 minutes, stirring occasionally.
4. Put 2½ cups of the soup in a blender or food processor and work for about 2 seconds, until roughly blended. Alternatively, mash with a potato masher.
5. Return the mixture to the saucepan, stir well, and cook the soup for 10 minutes over a low heat. Add salt to taste. Just before serving stir in the parsley, if using. Serve in warmed soup bowls.

6 oz bacon slices

1 tablespoon olive oil

1 onion, finely chopped

2 garlic cloves, finely chopped

2½ cups chicken stock

5 cups water

1½ lb potatoes, peeled and diced

3 leeks, trimmed, cleaned, and sliced

1 teaspoon chopped marjoram

½ teaspoon ground nutmeg

1 teaspoon Worcestershire sauce

3–4 tablespoons finely chopped flat-leaf parsley (optional)

salt and pepper

Serves 4 / Preparation time: 15 minutes, plus preparing the lobsters / Cooking time: 1 hour

Lobster and Corn Chowder

2 cooked lobsters, 1½ lb each

2 tablespoons butter

1 onion, finely chopped

1 carrot, finely chopped

1 celery stalk, finely chopped

1 sprig of thyme

1 sprig of parsley

2 bay leaves

4½ cups water

Chowder:

1 cup fresh corn kernels

2 tablespoons butter

1 small onion, chopped

1 small garlic clove, crushed

⅓ cup small strips pancetta

1¼ cups milk

1¼ cups light cream

2 lb potatoes, peeled and cut into ¾ inch cubes

cayenne pepper

4 tomatoes, peeled, seeded, and chopped

salt and pepper

1. Cut the lobsters in half lengthwise, remove and discard the grayish-green tomalley (the liver), the gills, and the intestinal vein running along the back. Smash the claws and remove the meat. Cut up the remaining meat. Place the shells in a plastic bag and smash into small pieces with a rolling pin.

2. Place the butter in a large saucepan and melt over a low heat. Add the onion, carrot, and celery and cook for 8–10 minutes, until soft.

3. Add the fresh herbs, water, and pieces of lobster shell. Bring to a boil, lower the heat, and simmer for 30 minutes. Strain.

4. To make the chowder, place two-thirds of the corn kernels in a blender or food processor with the strained lobster broth and work until smooth. Melt the butter in a large flameproof casserole, add the onion and garlic, and cook gently for 5 minutes.

5. Add the pancetta and cook until golden. Add the puréed corn mixture, the milk, cream, potatoes, and remaining corn kernels. Bring to a boil, lower the heat, and simmer for 10–15 minutes, until the potatoes are tender.

6. Season with salt, pepper, and cayenne. Stir in the chopped tomatoes and lobster meat. Heat through and serve.

FOOD FACT Fresh lobsters are available all year but are at their best and most plentiful in summer. They are generally available cooked and ready to eat. However, lobster flesh toughens easily, so unless it has been cooked very carefully, it may be a rubbery disappointment. Of a lobster's total weight, about one-quarter is edible meat.

Sweet Potato Soup

2 tablespoons butter or margarine

1 onion, chopped

2 carrots, sliced

2 celery stalks, sliced

1 bay leaf

1½ lb sweet potatoes, peeled and sliced

8 oz potatoes, peeled and sliced

5 cups chicken stock

150 ml (¼ pint) water

½ cup dry white wine

4–6 slices of bacon

¼ teaspoon grated nutmeg

¼ teaspoon white pepper

salt

chopped parsley, to garnish

1. Heat the butter or margarine in a skillet and cook the onion, carrots, celery, and bay leaf over a low heat for 5–8 minutes, stirring frequently.
2. Transfer the mixture to a saucepan. Add the sweet potatoes, potatoes, stock, water, and the white wine. Bring the mixture to a boil, then lower the heat and simmer, uncovered, for about 35–40 minutes, or until the vegetables are very tender. Remove the bay leaf.
3. Heat the bacon in a skillet over a gentle heat until the fat runs, then raise the heat and fry over a moderate heat until very crisp. Using tongs, transfer the bacon onto paper towels to drain.
4. In a blender or food processor, blend the mixture in batches until smooth, and transfer to a clean saucepan. Add the nutmeg, white pepper, and salt to taste. Place the pot over a moderate heat, stirring until the soup is hot.
5. Serve the soup in warmed bowls. Cut each bacon rasher into 2–3 pieces and divide among the bowls.

Serves 4–6 / Preparation time: 15 minutes / Cooking time: 40 minutes

Leek and Potato Soup

2 tablespoons butter

2 large leeks, trimmed, cleaned and finely sliced

8 oz potatoes, peeled and roughly diced

1 onion, roughly chopped

3 cups chicken stock or water

1¼ cups milk

salt and pepper

1 tablespoon snipped chives, to garnish

1. Melt the butter in a large saucepan, add the leeks, potatoes, and onion. Stir well to coat with the butter. Cover tightly with a piece of greaseproof paper and cook over a very gentle heat for about 15 minutes, until the vegetables have softened, stirring frequently, to prevent them from browning.
2. Add the chicken stock or water and milk and season with salt and pepper. Bring to the boil, lower the heat and simmer gently for about 20 minutes until the vegetables are tender.
3. Using a blender or food processor, purée the mixture in batches until smooth, and transfer to a clean saucepan.
4. Adjust the seasoning if necessary and when very hot, pour the soup into individual warmed bowls. Garnish with chives and serve.

Serves 4–6 / Preparation time: 20 minutes / Cooking time: 50–55 minutes

Red Pepper and Potato Soup

3 tablespoons olive oil

1 garlic clove, chopped

1 onion, chopped

2 red bell peppers, cored, seeded, and chopped

5 cups vegetable stock

½ teaspoon finely chopped fresh rosemary
   or ¼ teaspoon dried rosemary

¼ teaspoon sugar

2 tablespoons tomato paste

8 oz potatoes, peeled and chopped

salt and pepper

1. Heat the olive oil in a large saucepan. Add the garlic, onion, and red peppers and fry for 5 minutes, stirring frequently.

2. Add the vegetable stock, rosemary, sugar, and tomato paste. Stir well, then add the potatoes. Bring the mixture to a boil, lower the heat, and simmer, partially covered, for 40–45 minutes, or until the vegetables are very soft.

3. Using a blender or food processor, purée the mixture, in batches, until very smooth, and then transfer to a clean saucepan. Season with salt and pepper. Reheat gently and serve in warmed soup bowls.

Serves 6 / Preparation time: 15 minutes / Cooking time: 40 minutes

Caldo Verde

2 tablespoons olive oil

1 large onion, chopped

2 garlic cloves, chopped

1 lb potatoes, peeled and cut into 1-inch cubes

5 cups water or vegetable stock

8 oz collard greens, finely shredded

2 tablespoons chopped parsley

salt and pepper

croûtons, to serve (see page 24)

1. Heat the olive oil in a large skillet and fry the onion for 5 minutes, until softened but not brown. Add the garlic and potatoes and cook for a few minutes, stirring occasionally.
2. Add the water or stock, season with salt and pepper to taste, and cook for 15 minutes, until the potatoes are tender.
3. Mash the potatoes roughly in their liquid, then add the collard greens and boil, uncovered, for 10 minutes.
4. Add the parsley and simmer for 2–3 minutes, until heated through. Serve the soup with croûtons.

FOOD FACT Like many green vegetables, collard greens contain folic acid, or folate. Folate is necessary for normal cell growth and for the prevention of a particular form of anemia. The folate content of foods diminishes with storage, so choose leafy vegetables that are as fresh as possible.

2) Salads

Potato Salad with Dill Pickle and Anchovy

1½ lb salad potatoes, scrubbed
4 scallions, finely chopped
1 dill pickle, finely sliced
salt and pepper

Dressing:

6 tablespoons mayonnaise
3 tablespoons light cream
1 teaspoon Dijon mustard

To garnish:

anchovy fillets or strips of canned or
  bottled pimiento
2 tablespoons snipped chives

1. Cook the potatoes, whole and in their skins, in a large saucepan of boiling water for 10–15 minutes, or until tender. Drain and refresh under cold running water, then drain thoroughly and leave to cool.
2. Thickly slice the potatoes and place in a serving bowl with the chopped scallions and dill pickle. Add salt and pepper to taste.
3. To make the dressing, mix the mayonnaise, light cream, and mustard in a small bowl. Spoon the dressing over the potatoes and toss lightly to mix.
4. Serve the salad garnished with anchovy fillets or strips of pimiento and sprinkled with the snipped chives.

Serves 4 / Preparation time: 10 minutes / Cooking time: 10–15 minutes

Hot Potato Salad with Feta and Caper Vinaigrette

1½ lb small red-skinned potatoes, scrubbed
1 cup crumbled feta cheese

Caper vinaigrette:

1 tablespoon sherry vinegar
½ tablespoon Dijon mustard
2 tablespoons capers, drained and
　roughly chopped
1 tablespoon chopped tarragon
6 tablespoons extra virgin olive oil
salt and pepper

1. Cook the potatoes in a large saucepan of lightly salted boiling water for 10–15 minutes, or until just tender. Drain well. Cut the potatoes in half, if large.
2. To make the caper vinaigrette, mix together the vinegar, mustard, capers, and tarragon in a small bowl. Using a balloon whisk, gradually whisk in the olive oil in a steady stream until amalgamated, then season with salt and pepper.
3. Toss the warm potatoes with the vinaigrette and sprinkle with the crumbled feta.

FOOD FACT Capers are the small, green, unopened flower buds of a Mediterranean shrub. They are used, pickled, as a flavoring and as a garnish and are an essential ingredient in both Italian and Provençal cooking. They have a characteristic and slightly bitter flavor, which is developed by pickling.

Warm Salade Niçoise

It is impossible to give a definitive recipe for Niçoise salad, as there is much controversy as to what can and cannot be included in an authentic one. This one will be greeted with horror by any traditionalists, but it does make a very good dish.

about 8 oz small new potatoes, scrubbed, or
    medium potatoes, scrubbed and quartered

5 tablespoons extra virgin olive oil

2 tablespoons red wine vinegar

8 oz thin green beans or Haricot Vert, if
    available

8 oz fresh tuna steak, cut into wide strips

2 garlic cloves, finely chopped

2 anchovy fillets, chopped

about 1½ teaspoons Dijon mustard

1 red bell pepper, roasted, skinned, cored,
    seeded, and thinly sliced

2 tablespoons capers

salt and pepper

lemon wedges, to garnish (optional)

1. Steam the potatoes in a steamer or a colander set over a saucepan of boiling water for about 15–20 minutes, or until just tender. Transfer to a serving bowl and toss gently with 1 tablespoon each of the olive oil and red wine vinegar, and salt and pepper.
2. Steam the French beans in the same way for 5–6 minutes, until just tender. Set aside.
3. Heat 1 tablespoon of the oil in a nonstick skillet, add the strips of tuna, and sear evenly over a high heat. Add to the potato mixture.
4. Add the remaining oil to the skillet, then stir in the garlic and anchovies for 30 seconds. Stir in the remaining vinegar and boil for about 1 minute. Stir in the mustard, then pour over the potato mixture.
5. Add the pepper strips, steamed beans, capers, and more black pepper to the salad. Toss gently, taste, and adjust the seasoning, if necessary. Serve immediately, garnished with lemon wedges, if liked.

New Potato and Celery Salad

1 lb small new potatoes, scrubbed

6 celery stalks, with leaves if possible

½ cup black olives

3 tablespoons capers, rinsed and drained

few sprigs of parsley, roughly chopped

salt and pepper

Tarragon and lemon dressing:

2 tablespoons tarragon vinegar

1 teaspoon finely grated lemon zest

¼ teaspoon Dijon mustard

1 tablespoon chopped tarragon

5 tablespoons olive oil or grapeseed oil

salt and pepper

1. Cook the potatoes in a large saucepan of lightly salted boiling water for 10–15 minutes, until just tender. Drain and refresh under cold running water, then drain again thoroughly and leave to cool.
2. Slice the celery stalks diagonally and roughly chop any leaves. Place in a bowl with the olives, capers, and parsley. Add the cooled potatoes and season with salt and pepper.
3. To make the dressing, combine the vinegar, lemon zest, mustard, and tarragon in a small bowl. Add salt and pepper to taste. Stir to mix, then gradually whisk in the oil, using a balloon whisk. Alternatively, put all the ingredients in a screw-top jar, close the lid tightly, and shake well to combine.
4. Pour the dressing over the salad, toss well, and serve.

Warm Potato and Pancetta Salad

This aromatic potato salad is delicious on its own, as a side dish, or perhaps with one or two other root vegetable salads. When you cut the onions into wedges, leave the root ends intact so that the layers do not separate.

1 lb small new potatoes, scrubbed

2 red onions, cut into wedges, roots left intact

4 sprigs of rosemary

6 tablespoons extra virgin olive oil

3 oz pancetta, in thick slices, cut into strips

3 tablespoons red wine vinegar

coarse sea salt and pepper

1. Parboil the potatoes in a large saucepan of boiling water for 5 minutes. Drain thoroughly and transfer to a roasting pan. Preheat the oven to 400°F.
2. Add the red onion wedges to the roasting pan with the sprigs of rosemary. Drizzle over 4 tablespoons of the olive oil.
3. Place the roasting pan in the oven and roast for 45–minutes–1 hour, until the potatoes are tender and lightly patched with brown.
4. When the potatoes are cooked, heat the remaining olive oil in a skillet. Add the pancetta and fry until crisp and lightly browned. Add the red wine vinegar and bring to a boil, stirring, to deglaze the skillet. Pour over the potatoes and toss to coat. Season with coarse sea salt and pepper.
5. Serve warm or cold, discarding the rosemary stalks just before serving.

FOOD FACT Pancetta is cured belly of pork. It is evenly pink and white in color, and may be smoked or, more usually, air-dried and salt-cured. It must be cooked before eating. It is an important ingredient in Italian cuisine and there are many regional variations. Pancetta is widely used in pasta sauces, risottos, and bean casseroles.

Sweet Potato and Broiled Chile Salad

1½ lb sweet potatoes, peeled and sliced

3 large fresh red chiles

6 tablespoons peanut oil, for frying

a handful of cilantro, torn

coarse sea salt and pepper

lamb's lettuce or arugula, to serve

Dressing:

1 teaspoon finely grated lime zest

2 tablespoons lime juice

¼ cup peanut oil

2 tablespoons sesame oil

1. Parboil the sweet potato slices in a large saucepan of boiling water for about 5 minutes. Drain the potatoes well, then refresh under cold running water. Spread out on paper towels to dry.
2. Meanwhile, cook the chiles under a preheated hot broiler, turning them frequently, until the skins are blistered and blackened all over. Leave to cool slightly, then carefully remove and discard the skin and seeds. Cut the flesh into thin strips and set aside.
3. Heat half the peanut oil in a large skillet. Sauté the sweet potato slices in batches over a medium-high heat until crisp and lightly browned. Transfer to a large shallow serving bowl as they are done and add more oil to the skillet as necessary.
4. To make the dressing, mix all the ingredients together in a small bowl until thoroughly blended or shake together in a screw-top jar.
5. Add the strips of chile and the torn cilantro to the salad bowl. Season with coarse sea salt and pepper to taste. Toss lightly to mix.
6. Just before serving, pour the dressing over the sweet potatoes and chile, and toss well. Serve with lamb's lettuce or arugula.

3) Mashed Potatoes

Champ

Champ, also known as cally, poundies, and pandy, is one of the most famous ways of serving Ireland's best loved vegetable—the potato. Traditionally, champ would have been served as a main meal, with a glass of milk or buttermilk. Nowadays, however, it is used to accompany meats such as boiled ham and broiled sausages. Parsley, young nettle tops, peas, and fava beans can be substituted for the scallions.

2 lb potatoes, scrubbed

⅔ cup milk

4–5 scallions, finely chopped, plus extra, to garnish

¼–½ cup butter

salt and pepper

1. Cook the potatoes in a large saucepan of boiling water for about 20 minutes, or until tender.
2. Meanwhile, put the milk and chopped scallions into a saucepan. Bring to a boil and simmer for a few minutes. Keep warm.
3. When the potatoes are cooked, drain and return them to the pot. Dry them over a low heat, covered with a paper towel. Then, holding the warm potatoes in a dish towel, peel them carefully and mash well using a potato masher or fork.
4. Gradually beat the scallion-flavored milk into the mashed potatoes to form a soft but not sloppy mixture. Beat in half the butter and season with salt and pepper.
5. Divide the potatoes between 4 warmed plates or bowls and make a well in the center of each serving. Cut the remaining butter into four and put a piece in each of the servings. Serve immediately.

Creamy mashed potatoes

Choose old, floury potatoes. When cooked sufficiently, the potatoes should break under the pressure of a fork but not be mushy. Overcooking or cutting potatoes into small pieces makes them water-soaked and they lose flavor. Add hot milk for fluffy potatoes as cold milk makes them sticky.

6 potatoes, peeled
¼ cup butter, plus 1 tablespoon
⅓–⅔ cup hot milk
freshly grated nutmeg (optional)
salt and pepper

1. Cook the potatoes in a large saucepan of lightly salted boiling water until they are easily pierced with a skewer – about 20 minutes.
2. Drain, return to the saucepan and shake the pan over a low heat for a few minutes until the potatoes are thoroughly dry. Mash well with a potato masher or fork. Then, using a wooden spoon, beat until very smooth. Add the butter to the potatoes, then gradually beat in the hot milk until the potatoes are light and fluffy.
3. Season with salt and pepper, and a pinch of nutmeg, if liked.
4. To keep the potatoes hot after mashing, push them well down in the saucepan, packing the potato tightly. Level the top, add 1 tablespoon of butter, and spoon about 4 tablespoons of hot milk over the top. Cover and leave in a warm place. Before serving beat well, adding more hot milk if necessary. The potatoes will keep like this for up to 20 minutes.

Serves 4 / Preparation time: 15 minutes / Cooking time: 20 minutes

Horseradish Mashed Potatoes

1½ lb potatoes, peeled and cut into large chunks

¼ cup butter

⅔ cup light cream

2–3 tablespoons freshly grated or prepared horseradish

salt and pepper

1. Cook the potatoes in a large saucepan of boiling water for about 20 minutes, or until tender.
2. Drain the potatoes well, then return to the pan. Add the butter, light cream and horseradish and mash well with a potato masher or fork. Season with salt and pepper to taste and serve.

Mashed Potatoes with Garlic, Parsley and Olive Oil

Use firm, all-purpose or salad potatoes for this dish rather than baking potatoes, which are usually deemed essential for mashing.

2 lb potatoes, scrubbed

¼ cup extra virgin olive oil

¼ cup milk

3 large garlic cloves, crushed

¼ cup chopped flat-leaf parsley

salt and pepper

1. Cook the potatoes in a large saucepan of boiling water for about 20 minutes, or until tender. Drain well. As soon as they are cool enough to handle, peel the potatoes, then allow them to dry out in a clean pot over a gentle heat, stirring for a few moments.
2. Press the potatoes through a medium food mill back into the clean pot, and stir over a very low heat to dry out further still.
3. Warm the olive oil and milk together in a small saucepan, then stir in the crushed garlic. Beat into the potato purée, adding plenty of salt and pepper. When the potato is smooth and well seasoned, stir in the chopped parsley and transfer to a serving dish.

**Serves 4 / Preparation time: 15 minutes / Cooking time: 40 minutes /
Oven temperature: 325°F**

Roasted Garlic Mashed Potatoes

6 garlic cloves, unpeeled

2 tablespoons olive oil

1 tablespoon finely chopped rosemary or thyme

3 baking potatoes, total weight about 1½ lb,
    scrubbed and cut into small chunks

¼ cup butter

½ cup milk

salt and pepper

1. Preheat the oven to 325°F. Place the garlic cloves in a small ovenproof dish. Drizzle with the olive oil and sprinkle with the herbs. Cover with foil and bake for 35–40 minutes, until very soft.

2. Meanwhile, cook the potatoes in a large saucepan of boiling water for about 20 minutes, or until tender.

3. Remove the garlic from the oven and, when cooled, squeeze the cloves from their skins into a small bowl. Mash with a fork. Strain the oil from the baking dish over the garlic and mix well.

4. Combine the butter and milk in a small saucepan over a low heat and heat until the butter is melted. Drain the potatoes well when cooked, transfer to a warmed bowl, and mash well with a potato masher or fork.

5. Add the butter mixture to the potatoes and stir until smooth. Stir in the mashed roasted garlic and season with salt and pepper, to taste.

Serves 6–8 / Preparation time: 10 minutes / Cooking time: 20–25 minutes

Parmesan, Olive Oil and Pine Nut Mashed Potatoes

3 lb potatoes, peeled
⅔ cup olive oil, plus extra to serve
1 cup freshly grated Parmesan cheese
½ cup pine nuts, toasted, to serve
salt and pepper

1. Boil the potatoes in salted water for 15–20 minutes, until very tender. Drain and leave to steam in a colander for 5 minutes.
2. Press the potatoes through a potato ricer or mash them by hand. With an electric whisk, beat in the olive oil, then the Parmesan. Continue beating for a few minutes over the heat so that the mashed potato is nice and fluffy. Season well with salt and lots of pepper. Transfer to a warmed serving dish, drizzle with more oil, and scatter the pine nuts over the top.

Creamed Potatoes and Celery Root

1. Cook the potatoes and the celery root separately in large saucepans of lightly salted boiling water for about 20 minutes, or until tender. Drain well.

2. Purée the vegetables together using a blender or food processor or rub them through a sieve. Stir the pieces of butter into the hot vegetable purée. Blend in the sour cream or yogurt with plenty of freshly ground black pepper.

3. Put in a dish and serve garnished with toasted flaked almonds and a sprig of parsley. (This dish is ideal for making in advance. Just before serving, it can be reheated in a heatproof bowl set over a saucepan of boiling water, or in a microwave oven.)

2 lb potatoes, peeled and sliced
1 large celery root, peeled and sliced
¼ cup butter, cut into small pieces
⅔ cup sour cream or plain yogurt
salt and pepper

To garnish:
toasted flaked almonds
sprig of parsley

FOOD FACT Celery root, or celeriac, is the tuberous root of a plant belonging to the celery family. It has a milder sweeter taste than celery and is equally good cooked or used raw in salads. It needs to be peeled but tends to discolor when cut—this can be prevented by adding a few drops of lemon juice to the cooking water, or to the salad if being used raw. When cooked, the texture of celery root is similar to that of the potato, but with more bite to it.

Saffron Mashed Potatoes

Many potato varieties are suitable for this side dish. Mashing baking potatoes yields fluffy results; for a smoother, creamier texture, use white or red new potatoes. The mash is shown here with a bowl of saffron water.

2 lb potatoes, peeled and cut into large chunks
scant ½ cup light cream
large pinch of saffron threads
2 tablespoons boiling water
5 tablespoons extra virgin olive oil
salt and pepper

1. Cook the potatoes in a large saucepan of boiling water for about 20 minutes, or until tender.
2. Meanwhile, heat the cream to simmering point in a small saucepan, then remove from the heat. Place the saffron in a small bowl with the boiling water and leave to infuse for 10 minutes.
3. When the potatoes are cooked, drain well, return to the pan and add the cream, saffron water and olive oil. Mash together well with a potato masher or fork, season with salt and pepper to taste and serve.

Colcannon

Colcannon is similar to Champ (see page 54), but flavored, colored, and textured by the addition of cooked and shredded kale, a member of the cabbage family.

1 lb kale or green leaf cabbage, stalk removed,
   and finely shredded
1 lb potatoes, scrubbed
6 scallions or chives, finely chopped
⅔ cup milk or light cream
½ cup butter
salt and pepper

1. Cook the kale or cabbage and the potatoes separately in large saucepans of lightly salted boiling water and cook until tender—about 10–20 minutes for the kale or cabbage, longer for the potatoes.
2. Meanwhile, place the scallions or chives and the milk or cream in a small saucepan and simmer over a low heat for about 5 minutes.
3. Drain the kale or cabbage and mash with a fork.
4. Drain the potatoes. Holding them in a dish towel, peel them carefully while warm and mash well with a potato masher or fork. Add the hot milk and scallions, beating well to give a soft fluffy texture. Beat in the mashed kale or cabbage, season with salt and pepper, and add half the butter. The colcannon should be a speckled, green color.
5. Heat through thoroughly then serve in warmed individual dishes or bowls. Make a well in the center of each serving and put a knob of the remaining butter in each one. Serve immediately.

VARIATION An alternative method is to purée the cooked kale with the hot milk and scallions in a blender or food processor before adding to the potatoes. This produces an even texture and overall green color and makes an interesting variation.

4) Side Dishes

Serves 4 / Preparation time: 10 minutes / Cooking time: 25–30 minutes / Oven temperature: 450°F

Roast Potatoes with Rosemary and Garlic

1½ lb potatoes, scrubbed

¼ cup olive oil

2 tablespoons chopped rosemary

4 garlic cloves, sliced

salt and pepper

sprig of rosemary, to garnish

1. Preheat the oven to 450°F. Cut the potatoes lengthwise into quarters, and pat dry with paper towels.
2. Put half the olive oil in a large roasting pan, and place in the oven to warm through.
3. Mix the remaining oil and the rosemary in a large bowl and toss the potatoes in the oil to coat them completely.
4. Add the potatoes to the roasting pan in the oven, shake carefully to ensure an even layer of potatoes, then place the pan at the top of the oven and roast for 20 minutes.
5. Remove the pan from the oven and move the potatoes around so that they cook evenly. Scatter the garlic among the potatoes, return the pan to the oven and cook for a further 5 minutes. Remove the potatoes from the oven, season with salt and pepper, garnish with a sprig of rosemary and serve immediately.

Serves 4 / Preparation time: 15 minutes / Cooking time: 5–10 minutes

Potato and Cheese Croquettes

1 lb cooked mashed potatoes

1½ cups Gruyère, Stilton or Cheddar cheese,
    finely diced

1 egg yolk

3 tablespoons plain flour

1 egg, beaten

3 cups fresh bread crumbs

1 tablespoon freshly grated Parmesan cheese

sunflower oil or peanut oil, for frying

salt and pepper

1. Mix the potato with the cheese. Beat in the egg yolk and season with salt and pepper to taste. Shape the mixture into 16 croquettes.

2. Spread out the flour on a plate. Put the beaten egg on another shallow plate. Mix together the bread crumbs and Parmesan on another plate. Roll the croquettes in the flour, dip them in the beaten egg and coat them thoroughly in the bread crumb mixture. Arrange in a single layer on a plate and chill until ready to cook.

3. Heat about ½ inch of oil in a skillet and fry the croquettes, in batches, over a medium heat for about 5–10 minutes, turning constantly, so they cook evenly. When the croquettes are golden brown and crisp, remove them from the pan and drain them on paper towels. Serve hot.

Potato Galettes

2 lb potatoes, peeled and shredded

3 eggs

1 cup chopped onion

1 tablespoon flour

1 tablespoon chopped mixed parsley and chives

1 garlic clove, crushed

freshly grated nutmeg

6 tablespoons oil

salt and pepper

1. Place the shredded potatoes in a strainer and rinse well under cold running water to remove excess starch. Drain and transfer the potatoes to a bowl.

2. Break the eggs into the bowl of potatoes and mix together. Add the chopped onion, flour, herbs, and garlic. Season with salt, pepper, and a little grated nutmeg, and stir the mixture thoroughly.

3. Divide the potato mixture into even-sized portions and mold them into small cakes.

4. Heat the oil in a skillet. When it is hot, add the potato cakes and fry until golden brown and crisp on both sides, turning them once during cooking. Serve them very hot with a meat dish, or with charcuterie and a green salad.

Serves 4 / Preparation time: 10 minutes / Cooking time: 1–1¼ hours
Oven temperature: 400°F

Sesame Roast Potatoes

This is an exciting and elegant variation on the usual roast potato.

¼ cup olive oil
4 baking potatoes, about 6 oz each, peeled and halved lengthwise
2 tablespoons sesame seeds
salt

1. Preheat the oven to 400°F, then heat the oil in a roasting pan in the oven until hot.

2. Place the potatoes cut side down. Using a sharp knife, make cuts at ¼-inch intervals along the length of each potato almost through to the base, leaving just enough potato to hold the slices together.

3. Add the potatoes to the roasting pan and spoon the oil evenly over each one. Roast the potatoes for 30 minutes. Baste well and sprinkle with a little salt, if liked.

4. Sprinkle the potatoes with the sesame seeds and cook them for a further 30 minutes, or until the potatoes are golden brown and crisp. The cuts will open out a little during cooking to make an attractive fantail shape.

FOOD FACT Sesame seeds are the dried fruits of the sesame plant. The tiny pear-shaped seeds may be white, yellow, brown, or black, depending on the variety. They have a pleasant nutty flavor, which is developed by roasting, and yield an oil, which is used for cooking and in salads.

Serves 4 / Preparation time: 15 minutes / Cooking time: about 20 minutes

Almond Potatoes

12 oz potatoes, cooked and mashed with milk
   and butter
seasoned flour, for coating
1 egg, beaten
1 cup finely chopped almonds
2 tablespoons butter
1 tablespoon sunflower oil
sprigs of parsley, to garnish

1. Divide the mashed potato into 12 portions. Place the seasoned flour and chopped almonds
   on separate plates. Shape each portion of potato into a round patty, coating it with flour as
   you do so. Dip each potato patty in the beaten egg and then in the almonds.
2. Heat the butter and oil together in a large skillet and cook the potato patties a few at a
   time, for about 6 minutes, turning once, until golden. Drain on paper towels. Serve hot.

FOOD FACT Almonds are the seeds of a Mediterranean tree of the peach family, and one of the
most popular nuts worldwide. They have been cultivated since prehistoric times and
are the most important nut in commerce, with the United States being the main
producer, followed by Spain and Italy.

Serves 4–6 / Preparation time: 5 minutes / Cooking time: 55–60 minutes / Oven temperature: 425°F

Hot Fries

Use as little or as much chili powder as you like, to coat these oven-roasted fries.

4 large, even-sized potatoes
4–6 tablespoons olive oil
½ teaspoon salt
1–2 teaspoons chile powder or to taste
chilli flakes, to garnish
sour cream or mayonnaise, to serve

1. Preheat the oven to 425°F. Cut each potato into 8 wedges and place in a large bowl. Add the oil, salt, and chili powder, and toss until evenly coated.
2. Transfer the wedges to a baking sheet and bake for 15 minutes. Turn over and cook for a further 15 minutes, then turn once more and cook for a final 25–30 minutes, until crisp and golden.
3. Cool slightly, garnish with chile flakes and serve with either sour cream or mayonnaise.

**Serves 2–4 / Preparation time: 15 minutes / Cooking time: 1–1¼ hours /
Oven temperature: 350°F then 400°F**

Potatoes Dauphinoise

1 lb potatoes, peeled and thinly sliced

3 tablespoons butter

1 large garlic clove, crushed

1¼ cups heavy cream

salt and pepper

fresh red and green chiles, deseeded and
   finely sliced, to garnish (optional)

cooked green beans or Haricot Vert, if available,
   to serve

1. Preheat the oven to 350°F. Wash the
   sliced potatoes and pat dry with paper
   towels. Use the butter to grease an
   ovenproof dish. Scatter crushed garlic
   over the dish and fill with layers of
   potato slices.
2. Pour the cream over the potatoes and
   sprinkle with salt and pepper. Place
   the dish in the oven and bake for
   1–1¼ hours, or until the potatoes are
   tender when pierced with a skewer.
3. Increase the heat to 400°F. for the last
   10 minutes to brown the top.
4. Garnish with the chiles, if using, and
   serve hot with French beans.

Serves 4 / Preparation time: 20 minutes, plus soaking / Cooking time: 45 minutes / Oven temperature: 350°F

Genoese Mushrooms and Potatoes

In this Ligurian recipe the potatoes absorb the flavor of the mushrooms, making it seem as if there are more mushrooms than there actually are.

1 cup dried porcini

1¼ cups hot water

12 oz mushrooms, preferably chestnut, thinly sliced

1 lb potatoes, thinly sliced

4 garlic cloves, crushed

leaves from a bunch of basil

olive oil, for brushing

salt and pepper

1. Soak the dried mushrooms in a bowl containing the hot water for 30 minutes. Drain, straining the liquid through cheesecloth or a filter paper. Simmer the rehydrated mushrooms in the strained soaking liquid until the liquid has evaporated. Toss with the fresh mushrooms, potatoes, garlic, basil, and salt and pepper.

2. Preheat the oven to 350°F. Oil an ovenproof dish that will hold the potatoes and mushrooms in a layer no more than about 1½ inches deep. Spread the vegetable mixture evenly in the dish.

3. Bake for about 45 minutes, until the potatoes are tender, turning the ingredients over about halfway through cooking. Leave to stand for a couple of minutes before serving.

Potato Cakes

1 lb potatoes, peeled and
   shredded
1 onion, chopped
2 tablespoons chopped parsley
2 eggs, beaten
2 tablespoons olive oil
salt and pepper

1. Place the shredded potatoes in a strainer and rinse well under cold running water to remove excess starch. Drain.
2. Place the potatoes in a bowl with the onion, parsley, eggs, and salt and pepper to taste. Mix thoroughly and divide into rounds.
3. Heat the oil in an 8–9-inch heavy-based skillet. Add the potato cakes, in batches, and pat lightly. Fry them gently for about 8–10 minutes, until the undersides are crisp and brown, then fry the other side for 10 minutes, until crisp and brown.
4. Season with salt and pepper and serve immediately.

Serves 4 / Preparation time: 10 minutes, plus cooling / Cooking time: 40–45 minutes / Oven temperature: 400°F

Roasted New Potatoes with Smoked Salmon and Caviar

This is a delicious combination, well worth the time spent assembling.

16 small new potatoes, about 1½ oz each, scrubbed but left unpeeled

2 tablespoons olive oil

1 tablespoon chopped rosemary

1 tablespoon chopped sage

125 g (4 oz) crème fraîche

125 g (4 oz) smoked salmon, cut into strips

25 g (1 oz) lumpfish caviar

1 tablespoon snipped chives

sea salt and pepper

lemon wedges, to serve (optional)

1. Place the potatoes in a small roasting pan, add the olive oil, herbs and some sea salt and toss well. Put the roasting tin on the top shelf of a preheated oven, 400°F and roast for 40–45 minutes, stirring occasionally, until the potatoes are crisp on the outside and very soft in the centre.
2. Remove the potatoes from the oven and leave to cool for 5 minutes.
3. Cut a cross in the top of each potato and press open slightly. Transfer to a serving plate and top each with a spoonful of crème fraîche, a piece of smoked salmon, a little caviar and snipped chives.
4. Serve at once with plenty of freshly ground black pepper and lemon wedges, if liked.

Emmentaler Potato Fritters

1 lb potatoes, peeled and grated

2 tablespoons plain flour

1 egg, beaten

1 onion, chopped

1 garlic clove, crushed

2 cups Emmentaler cheese, grated

salt and pepper

To garnish:

basil leaves

snipped chives

To serve:

grilled bacon

torn radicchio leaves

1. Place the grated potato on a clean tea towel, gather up the corners and twist into a tight ball to extract all the excess moisture from the potato. This is important otherwise the fritters will be soggy.
2. Mix together the flour and egg in a bowl, until smooth. Add the potato and the remaining ingredients, season with sea salt and pepper with salt and pepper and mix well.
3. Heat a grill pan. Divide the mixture into 8 and place 4 portions of fritter mixture on the grill. Flatten with a palette knife and cook for 4–5 minutes, then turn and cook for a further 4–5 minutes. Do not disturb the fritters while they are cooking as a crust needs to form on the cooking side, or they will be difficult to turn.
4. Keep the grilled fritters warm while you cook the remainder. Garnish with basil and snipped chives. Serve as a delicious side dish or with grilled bacon and radicchio, as a starter.

Serves 4 / Preparation time: 10 minutes / Cooking time: 10 minutes

Home-fried Potatoes

6 tablespoons butter or margarine
1½ lb cooked potatoes, fairly thickly
   sliced
sea salt
chopped thyme, to garnish

1. Heat the butter or margarine in a large skillet. Add the potatoes and sauté gently for about 10 minutes, turning them often until golden brown on both sides.
2. Sprinkle with sea salt and thyme just before serving.

Barbecued Potato Wedges with Sun-dried Tomato Aïoli

4 large potatoes, scrubbed

¼ cup olive oil

paprika, for sprinkling

coarse sea salt, for sprinkling

Sun-dried tomato aïoli:

4–6 garlic cloves, crushed

2 egg yolks

2 tablespoons lemon juice, plus extra to taste

1¼ cups extra virgin olive oil

8 sun-dried tomato halves in oil, drained and
   finely chopped

salt and pepper

1. If using wooden skewers, soak them in cold water for 30 minutes.

2. Cook the whole potatoes, in their skins, in a large saucepan of boiling water for about 20 minutes, or until just tender. Drain, and when cool enough to handle, cut each potato into large wedges.

3. To make the sun-dried tomato aïoli, place the garlic and egg yolks in a blender or food processor, add the lemon juice, and mix briefly. With the motor running, gradually add the oil in a thin stream until the mixture forms a thick cream. Scrape into a bowl and stir in the sun-dried tomatoes. Season with salt and pepper and add extra lemon juice to taste, if necessary.

4. Brush the potato wedges with the olive oil, sprinkle with a little paprika and coarse sea salt, and skewer or lay the potato wedges on a hot barbecue grill. Cook for 5–6 minutes, turning frequently, until golden brown all over. Serve with the aïoli.

Makes 8 / Preparation time: 25 minutes / Cooking time: 35–40 minutes / Oven temperature: 425°F

Salmon and Potato Parcels

8 oz potatoes, peeled

1 tablespoon butter

½ onion, finely chopped

¼ teaspoon fennel seeds, roughly ground

1 teaspoon finely grated lemon zest

1 tablespoon chopped dill

6 oz smoked salmon, finely chopped

1 tablespoon lemon juice

1 egg yolk

1 lb puff pastry, defrosted if frozen

salt and pepper

flour, for dusting

Egg glaze:

1 small egg

1 tablespoon milk

pinch of salt

1. Cook the potatoes in a large saucepan of lightly salted boiling water for about 20 minutes, or until tender.
2. Meanwhile, melt the butter in a small saucepan and fry the onion, fennel seeds, and lemon zest for 10 minutes, until very soft. Transfer to a bowl.
3. Drain the cooked potatoes well and mash with a fork—the texture of the mashed potato should remain fairly rough. Add the potato, dill, smoked salmon, lemon juice, and egg yolk to the onion in the bowl, and mix until well blended. Season with salt and pepper.
4. Preheat the oven to 425°F. Roll out the puff pastry on a lightly floured surface to form a thin rectangle 7 x 14 inches. Cut into 8 squares measuring 3½ inches.
5. Divide the filling among the squares, placing a mound of filling slightly off center on each pastry square. Dampen the edges of the pastry and fold each one in half diagonally to form a triangle. Press the edges together to seal.
6. Transfer the pastry triangles to a lightly greased baking sheet. Beat together the ingredients for the egg glaze and brush the glaze lightly over the pastry. Bake for 15–20 minutes, until puffed up and golden. Serve hot.

Serves 4 / Preparation time: 25 minutes, plus salting and resting / Cooking time: 55–60 minutes / Oven temperature: 350°F

Eggplant and Potato Bake

3 eggplants

5–6 tablespoons olive oil

2 onions, chopped

3 garlic cloves, crushed

4 large sun-ripened tomatoes, peeled, seeded, and chopped

2–3 sprigs of oregano or marjoram

2 large potatoes, cut into slices

sugar to taste (optional)

2 red bell peppers, cored, seeded, and sliced

salt and pepper

crusty bread, to serve

1. Quarter the eggplants lengthwise, then halve each piece crosswise. Place in a strainer, sprinkle evenly with salt, and leave for 30–minutes–1 hour, to drain.

2. Make a tomato sauce by heating about 2 tablespoons of oil in a saucepan. Add the onions and garlic, and fry gently until softened and lightly browned. Stir in the tomatoes and oregano or marjoram and simmer for about 15 minutes.

3. Meanwhile, heat a thin layer of oil in a large skillet, add a single layer of potato slices, and cook over a moderate heat until golden on both sides and about three-quarters cooked. Remove with a slotted spoon, drain on paper towels, then place in a flameproof casserole. Repeat with the remaining potatoes.

4. Season the tomato sauce with salt and pepper, to taste, and add a little sugar if necessary. Pour about one-third over the potatoes.

5. Rinse and pat dry the eggplant pieces, then fry in batches in the skillet, adding more oil as necessary, until golden. Using a slotted spoon, transfer to paper towels to drain, then add to the casserole. Pour over another third of the tomato sauce.

6. Fry the red pepper slices in the skillet, then add to the casserole. Pour over the remaining tomato sauce. Almost cover the casserole, leaving a small gap for steam to escape. Simmer very gently for 15–20 minutes, until the potatoes are tender and the sauce thick. Alternatively, bake, uncovered, in a preheated oven at 350°F for 15 minutes.

7. Let stand for 5–10 minutes before serving or cool to room temperature. Serve with plenty of crusty bread to mop up the juices.

Moroccan Potatoes with Harissa, Peppers, and Tomatoes

3 tablespoons olive oil

1½ lb potatoes, cut into chunks

1 large onion, sliced

2 red bell peppers, cored, seeded, and sliced

1 yellow bell pepper, cored, seeded, and sliced

4 well-flavored tomatoes, cut into chunks

3 garlic cloves, crushed

3–4 teaspoons Harissa (see page 21)

salt

1. Heat 1 tablespoon of the oil in a large skillet. Add the potatoes, stir to coat them in the oil, then cover the skillet and fry over a low heat for 15 minutes, shaking the skillet occasionally.

2. Add the remaining oil to the skillet, then add the onion and red and yellow peppers. Increase the heat and cook, uncovered, for 10 minutes, stirring frequently, until the peppers have browned.

3. Add the tomatoes and garlic and continue to cook for about 4 minutes, until the tomatoes have softened. Add the harissa, season with salt, and serve.

Serves 5–10 / Preparation time: 10 minutes, plus chilling / Cooking time: 1 hour 25 minutes / Oven temperature: 400°F

Potato Skins with Sour Cream Dip

5 large baking potatoes, scrubbed and dried

⅔ cup sour cream

1 teaspoon snipped chives, plus extra, to garnish

sunflower oil, for frying

salt and pepper

1. Preheat the oven to 400°F. Prick the potatoes with a fork. Place directly on the oven rack and bake for about 1¼ hours, or until soft.
2. Meanwhile, prepare the dip. Mix the sour cream in a bowl with the snipped chives. Season with salt and pepper, to taste. Cover the bowl and leave to chill.
3. When the potatoes are cooked, cool for a few minutes, then cut each one into quarters lengthwise. Scoop out most of the potato flesh, leaving a thin layer next to the skin. (Reserve the scooped-out potato for use in another recipe.)
4. Pour the oil into a small deep skillet to a depth of 3 inches. Heat the oil to 375°F, or until a cube of bread browns in 30 seconds. Carefully add a few potato skins to the hot oil and cook, in batches, for about 2 minutes, until brown and crisp. Remove and drain on paper towels.
5. To serve, arrange the potato skins on a plate with the dip, sprinkled with extra chives, in the center.

Beef and Potato Curry Puffs

1¼ lb shortcrust pastry, defrosted if frozen

oil, for deep-frying

Filling:

1 tablespoon vegetable oil

1 small onion, finely chopped

2 garlic cloves, crushed

1 teaspoon grated fresh ginger root

1 small fresh red chile, seeded and
    finely chopped

2 tablespoons medium curry paste

1 cup ground beef

½ teaspoon salt

1 cup finely diced cooked potatoes

1. Start by making the filling. Heat the vegetable oil in a heavy-based skillet, add the onion, garlic, ginger, and chile, and fry over a gentle heat, stirring constantly, for about 5 minutes, until softened. Stir in the curry paste and fry for about 1 minute, until fragrant.

2. Stir in the ground beef and salt, mix well, and fry for 5 minutes, stirring occasionally. Stir in the diced potato and cook for a further 2 minutes. Taste, add more salt if necessary, then leave the beef filling to cool.

3. Roll out the pastry thinly on a lightly floured surface. Using a pastry cutter, stamp out 24 x 4-inch circles and place 1 heaped teaspoon of beef filling on one half of each circle. Dampen the pastry edges with water and fold over each pastry circle to produce semi-circles. Press the edges together to seal.

4. Heat the oil for deep-frying in a saucepan. Deep-fry the curry puffs in batches, allowing 5–6 minutes for each batch and turning halfway through cooking, until they are crisp and golden. (Do not allow the oil to get too hot or the pastry will burn.)

5. Remove the puffs from the pot with a slotted spoon and drain on paper towels. Leave to cool slightly and serve warm or cold, as liked.

Serves 4 / Preparation time: 5 minutes, plus cooling / Cooking time: 30–35 minutes / Oven temperature: 400°F

Potatoes Wrapped in Prosciutto

12 small new potatoes, scrubbed
   but unpeeled
12 very thin slices of prosciutto
2 tablespoons olive oil
sea salt

1. Cook the potatoes in a large saucepan of boiling water for 10–15 minutes, or until tender. Drain well and allow to go cold.
2. Roll each cooked potato in a slice of prosciutto, patting with your hands to mold the ham to the shape of the potato.
3. Preheat the oven to 400°F. Brush a roasting pan with the oil. Add the ham-wrapped potatoes and bake for 20 minutes. Keep an eye on the potatoes while they are cooking, as they may need turning, or moving around—often the ones on the edge get more color than the ones in the middle.
4. Serve the potatoes sprinkled with sea salt.

FOOD FACT Prosciutto is a good-quality raw, dry-cured, ham from Italy. It is lightly salted and is probably best recognized as the transparently thin slices that are often served with fresh melon or figs as an appetizer.

Rösti

With its crisp golden crust and soft stringy center, this Swiss potato pancake is very easy to make. The dish originated as a way of using up leftover cooked potatoes. The secret of a good rösti is to shred the potatoes when cold, which keeps the potato strands separate. Serve with broiled sausages, liver and onions, or baked fish, or serve it topped with a fried egg or with a tomato sauce.

2 lb even-sized baking potatoes, scrubbed but
   unpeeled
6 tablespoons butter
1 small mild onion, very finely chopped
salt and pepper

1. Cook the potatoes in a large saucepan of lightly salted boiling water for about 7 minutes. Drain well. When the potatoes are quite cold, peel them and shred them coarsely into a large bowl.
2. Heat 1 tablespoon of the butter in a large, heavy-based skillet. Add the onion and cook for about 5 minutes, until soft. Stir into the shredded potato and season with salt and pepper.
3. Melt the remaining butter in the skillet. Set aside about 1 tablespoon of the melted butter in a cup. Add the potato mixture to the skillet and form into a neat cake. Cook gently for about 15 minutes, or until the underside of the cake is a crusty golden brown, shaking the skillet occasionally so that the rösti cake does not stick.
4. To cook the top of the rösti, pour over the reserved melted butter and either place the skillet under a preheated broiler to brown, or turn the rösti over in the skillet and brown.
5. To serve, invert the rösti cake onto a warmed flat dish and cut it into wedges.

Serves 4 / Preparation time: 5 minutes / Cooking time: 35–40 minutes / Oven temperature: 425°F

Roasted Paprika Potato Wedges

4 large baking potatoes, about
   8 oz each, left unpeeled
¼ cup olive or sunflower oil
1–2 teaspoons paprika
salt
sour cream mixed with chives, or
   mayonnaise, to serve

1. Preheat the oven to 425°F. Scrub the potatoes well, rinse under cold running water, and pat dry with a dish towel. Cut each potato lengthwise into 8 wedges.
2. Place the potato wedges in a roasting pan, drizzle over the oil, and toss well to coat. Sprinkle over the paprika and season with salt. Place the potatoes in the top of the oven and roast them for 35–40 minutes, basting with the oil 2–3 times during cooking, until they are tender and nicely browned.
3. Serve the wedges as an appetizer with a bowl of sour cream mixed with snipped chives, or with mayonnaise, or as a side dish to replace traditional roast potatoes or fries.

Serves 4 / Preparation time: 10–15 minutes / Cooking time: about 30 minutes

Grilled Warm New Potatoes with Fresh Mint Dressing

This makes a wonderful, fresh-tasting accompaniment to lamb chops.

1½ lb small new potatoes, scrubbed and
   halved lengthwise
mint leaves, to garnish

Dressing:
finely grated zest and juice of 2 limes
½ cup grapeseed oil
2 tablespoons chopped mint
coarse sea salt and pepper

1. Place a layer of potato slices in a preheated hot grill pan and cook for 6 minutes on each side, reducing the heat as required. Remove and keep warm while cooking the remaining potato slices.

2. Combine the lime zest and juice and the oil in a small pitcher, beating well with a whisk. Add the sea salt, pepper and chopped mint and whisk until evenly combined. Alternatively, place all the dressing ingredients in a screw-top jar and shake to combine thoroughly.

3. Toss the cooked potatoes in the dressing, pile into a serving dish, and serve garnished with mint leaves.

Serves 4 / Preparation time: 5 minutes, plus soaking / Cooking time: 10–15 minutes

Perfect French Fries

4 potatoes, peeled

sunflower oil, for deep-frying

sea salt

1. Thinly slice the potatoes crosswise, using a sharp knife, a mandolin, or the slicing blade of a food processor. Soak the slices in ice-cold water for 15–20 minutes to remove the excess starch and to crisp the potatoes.
2. Drain the potato slices and dry them thoroughly on a clean dish towel or paper towels.
3. Heat the oil for deep-frying to 375°F, or until a cube of bread browns in 30 seconds. Place a few potato slices in the frying basket and lower it into the oil. Cook for 3–5 minutes, until the fries are golden brown, turning if necessary. Remove the basket and drain the fries on paper towels. Repeat with the remaining potato slices.
4. Serve the fries sprinkled with sea salt.

Serves 6 / Preparation time: 25 minutes / Cooking time: 45 minutes / Oven temperature: 400°F

Parsnip Duchesse Potatoes

1½ lb parsnips, peeled and cut into even-sized pieces

1½ lb potatoes, peeled and cut into even-sized pieces

pinch of ground nutmeg

1 egg, beaten

salt and pepper

1. Cook the parsnips and potatoes separately in large saucepans of lightly salted boiling water for about 20 minutes, or until tender. Preheat the oven to 400°F.
2. Drain the vegetables well, then mash together using a potato masher or fork. Beat until smooth, then rub through a sieve. Turn the purée into a bowl, season well with salt and pepper, and beat in the nutmeg and egg.
3. Spoon the vegetable mixture into a pastry bag fitted with a large star tip and pipe large whirls of the mixture onto a greased baking sheet.
4. Bake for about 25 minutes until lightly browned. Serve hot.

**Serves 4 / Preparation time: 15 minutes / Cooking time: 1–1½ hours /
Oven temperature: 425°F then 350°F**

Baked Cheese Soufflé Potatoes

4 baking potatoes, scrubbed

1 cup grated Gruyère cheese

freshly grated nutmeg

½ cup butter

¼ cup heavy cream

2 eggs, separated

salt and pepper

1. Preheat the oven to 425°F. Prick the potatoes with a fork. Place them directly on the oven rack and bake for about 1 hour, or until the potatoes feel soft. Remove the potatoes from the oven and lower the oven temperature to 350°F.

2. Using a sharp kitchen knife, slice each potato in half lengthwise. Scoop the soft potato flesh into a mixing bowl. Arrange the potato shells on a baking sheet and return to the oven to crisp them.

3. Mash the scooped-out potato with a fork. Mix in the grated cheese, a seasoning of salt and pepper, and a grating of nutmeg. Add the butter, cream, and egg yolks to the potato mixture and beat with a wooden spoon, until smooth and soft.

4. Place the egg whites in a clean bowl and whisk them into stiff peaks. Fold them carefully into the potato mixture with a metal tablespoon. Pile the mixture back into the potato skins and return to the oven for 20–25 minutes, or until golden, before serving.

Potato Herb Biscuits

12 oz potatoes, peeled and cut into even-sized
pieces

1 tablespoon butter

2 tablespoons snipped chives

2 tablespoons chopped parsley

¾ cup plain or whole-wheat flour

a little milk (optional)

flour, for dusting

sunflower oil, for frying

salt and pepper

1. Cook the potatoes in a large saucepan of lightly salted boiling water for about 20 minutes, or until tender. Drain.

2. Place the potatoes in a bowl and mash with the butter. Add salt and pepper to taste and stir in the chives and parsley. Beat in the flour. Add a little milk if the mixture is dry.

3. Form the potato mixture into a ball and divide into 8 rounds. Roll each one out on a lightly floured surface to a thickness of about ¼ inch. Prick the surface all over with a fork.

4. Lightly oil a heavy-based skillet. Heat the skillet, then cook the potato biscuits, a few at a time, for 3 minutes on each side, until golden brown.

Boxty Pancakes

Sometimes referred to as "stamp," this is a traditional Irish potato dish, found in the northern counties of Cavan, Donegal, Leitrim, and Monaghan.

2 tablespoons all-purpose flour

1 teaspoon baking powder

1 lb potatoes, peeled and shredded

⅔ cup milk

oil, for frying

salt and pepper

butter, jam or fried bacon, to serve

1. Sift the flour into a bowl with the baking powder.
2. Place the shredded potatoes in another bowl and add the flour. Season with salt and pepper and stir in the milk.
3. Drop tablespoons of this mixture onto a hot, lightly oiled skillet. Cook for about 5 minutes on each side, until golden brown. Serve hot, with butter and jam or with fried bacon.

**Makes a 500 g (1 lb) loaf / Preparation time: 15 minutes, plus rising / Cooking time: 30 minutes
Oven temperature: 400°F then 350°F**

Roquefort Bread

4 cups strong all-purpose white flour, plus extra,
   for dusting
2 teaspoons salt
2 tablespoons butter, plus extra, for greasing
2 teaspoons fast-acting dry yeast
⅔ cup lukewarm milk
1 cup sieved cooked potato
1 cup crumbled Roquefort or other blue cheese
beaten egg, to glaze

1. Sift the flour with the salt into a warmed bowl. Rub in the butter until the mixture resembles fine bread crumbs. Stir in the yeast. Stir the milk into the sieved potato in another bowl, then work this mixture into the flour to make a soft but not sticky dough. Knead on a lightly floured surface for 5 minutes, then knead in the crumbled cheese.
2. Grease a 1 lb-loaf pan. Shape the dough to fit the pan, or shape into a round cob shape and place on a greased baking sheet. Cover with wax paper and leave to rise in a warm place for 30 minutes, or until the loaf has doubled in size. Preheat the oven to 400°F.
3. Brush the loaf with beaten egg and bake for 15 minutes. Lower the heat to 350°F and bake for a further 15 minutes. Turn the loaf out of the pan, if using, and leave to cool on a wire rack.

**Makes 6 / Preparation time: 5–10 minutes, plus cooking and mashing potatoes /
Cooking time: 5 minutes**

Irish Potato Bread

This Irish potato bread is cooked on a cast-iron griddle or in a
heavy-based skillet, which is heated gently without fat or oil,
only a light dusting of flour before using.

8 oz potatoes, cooked, mashed, and still warm
½ teaspoon salt
2 tablespoons butter, melted
½ cup all-purpose flour, plus extra for dusting.

1. Place the potatoes in a large bowl and mix in the salt and melted butter. Stir in the flour
   to make a pliable dough. Turn onto a lightly floured surface and roll into a round, about
   ¼-inch thick and 9 inches in diameter. Cut into 6 triangular shapes (called "farls").
2. Lightly dust a cast-iron griddle or heavy-based skillet with flour and heat it. When the flour
   begins to turn a pale beige, the temperature is right for cooking. Arrange the farls on the
   griddle or skillet and cook for about 2½ minutes on each side, until lightly browned.
3. Serve them hot with butter and sugar or jam. Alternatively, the cooked bread may be fried
   and eaten with bacon, sausages, and egg as part of a cooked breakfast.

TIP Potato bread is best made while the
potatoes are still hot. If using leftovers,
heat for 30 seconds in a microwave oven
before mixing with the rest of the
ingredients. Instead of making farls, you
could cut the potato bread into 10 circles,
using a 3-inch plain cutter.

Serves 4 / Preparation time: 10 minutes / Cooking time: 35 minutes / Oven temperature: 450°F

Potato Bravas

2 lb small potatoes, scrubbed

2 tablespoons olive oil

sea salt

Sauce:

¼ cup olive oil

2 tablespoons water

1 tablespoon tomato paste

1 tablespoon red wine vinegar

1 teaspoon chile sauce

2 teaspoons paprika

salt and pepper

Potato Bravas is a fiercely hot tapas dish, characterized by the use of paprika.

1. Preheat the oven to 450°F. Cut the potatoes into ½-inch thick slices and place in a single layer on a large baking sheet.

2. Brush with olive oil, sprinkle with sea salt and bake for 20 minutes. Turn the potatoes over and bake for a further 10 minutes, until crisp.

3. Meanwhile, combine all the sauce ingredients in a sauté pan. Add the cooked potatoes and heat through. Season with salt and pepper to taste and serve hot.

5 Main Meals

Gnocchi with Pesto

If made properly, these dumplings from northern Italy will be as light as a feather. The secret is to use baking potatoes, cook them in their skins, and mix the dough while still warm. A light hand is needed, and as little flour as possible.

Gnocchi:

2 lb baking potatoes, scrubbed

1 teaspoon salt

¼ cup butter

1 egg, beaten

2–2½ cups all-purpose white flour

all-purpose white or semolina flour, for sprinkling

Pesto sauce:

2 cups roughly chopped basil leaves

2 tablespoons roughly chopped pine nuts

2 garlic cloves

¼ cup olive oil

juice of ½ lemon

⅓ cup freshly grated Parmesan cheese

salt and pepper

To serve:

3 tablespoons butter, plus extra, for greasing

freshly grated Parmesan cheese

1. Cook the potatoes in a large saucepan of boiling water for 20–30 minutes, or until tender.
2. Meanwhile, make the pesto sauce. Put the basil and pine nuts in a mortar with the garlic and season with salt and pepper. Pound together until reduced to a thick paste. Transfer to a bowl. Add the oil, a little at a time, stirring constantly, until thick. Stir in the lemon juice and grated Parmesan, cover, and set aside.
3. Drain the cooked potatoes well. Holding the warm potatoes in a dish towel, peel and pass them through a potato ricer or sieve into a bowl.
4. While the potatoes are still warm, add the salt, butter, beaten egg, and half of the plain flour. Lightly mix together, then turn out onto a lightly floured surface. Gradually knead the rest of the flour into the dough until it is smooth, soft, and a little sticky.
5. Roll the dough into long "sausages" about 1-inch thick, and cut them into ¾-inch pieces. Take each piece and press it over the back of a fork with your floured thumb so that the gnocchi have ridges on one side and an indentation on the other. Spread the gnocchi out on a dish towel sprinkled with all-purpose white or semolina flour.
6. Cook the gnocchi, a few at a time, in a large saucepan of lightly salted, gently boiling water for 2–3 minutes, or until they rise to the surface. Remove from the pot with a slotted spoon and place in a buttered serving dish. Dot with the butter and pour the pesto sauce over the top. Serve immediately, sprinkled with grated Parmesan.

FOOD FACT Pesto is a sauce originating from Genoa in Italy. The main ingredients are garlic, pine nuts, fresh basil, and grated Parmesan, which are pounded together to make a thick creamy paste. Commercial bottled versions are available but do not compare with homemade pesto, which is redolent with fresh basil and can easily be made in a food processor.

Carnival Chicken with Sweet Mashed Potatoe

4 skinless chicken breasts, about 5 oz each

sprigs of flat-leaf parsley, to garnish

Marinade:

7 tablespoons sweet sherry

1 teaspoon Angostura bitters

1 tablespoon light soy sauce

1 tablespoon chopped fresh ginger root

pinch of ground cumin

pinch of ground coriander

1 teaspoon dried mixed herbs

1 small onion, finely chopped

5 tablespoons fresh chicken stock

Mashed Sweet Potatoes:

2 sweet potatoes, scrubbed

2 tablespoons farmer's cheese (optional)

salt and pepper

1. Place the chicken breasts in a nonmetallic dish. Mix all the marinade ingredients together in a bowl. Spoon over the chicken, making sure the pieces are well coated. Cover and leave to marinate in the refrigerator overnight.
2. When you are ready to cook, place the marinated chicken breasts on a broiler pan and cook under a preheated medium broiler for 20 minutes, turning them over halfway through cooking.
3. Meanwhile, cook the sweet potatoes in their skins in a large saucepan of boiling water for 20 minutes, until soft. Drain well, then, holding the warm potatoes in a dish towel, peel them carefully. Mash the potato using a potato masher or fork and let it dry off a bit before stirring in the farmer's cheese, if using. Season with salt and pepper and serve with the chicken. Garnish with the flat-leaf parsley.

Serves 4 / Preparation time: 35 minutes, plus infusing and cooling / Cooking time: 40 minutes / Oven temperature: 400°F

1½ cups frozen or fresh mixed diced vegetables

butter, for frying

1½ cups sliced mushrooms

1 large or 2 medium onions, thinly sliced

¾ cup shredded Cheddar cheese

1 egg yolk, beaten

salt and pepper

Potato pastry:

2 cups self-rising flour

¾ cup butter or soft margarine

1 teaspoon salt

1 cup cold, cooked mashed potato

1 tablespoon milk

Béchamel sauce:

⅔ cup milk

½ small onion, roughly chopped

1 bay leaf

1 tablespoon butter

2 tablespoons all-purpose flour

Vegetable Pie with Potato Pastry

1. Begin by infusing the milk for the béchamel sauce. Put the milk, onion, and bay leaf in a small saucepan. Heat gently until just boiling. Remove the pot from the heat and set aside for 20 minutes for the flavors to infuse.

2. To make the potato pastry, place the flour in a bowl, add the butter or margarine, and rub in using your fingertips. Mix in the salt and work the mashed potato into the mixture, adding the 1 tablespoon of milk a little at a time.

3. Preheat the oven to 400°F. Turn the dough onto a lightly floured surface and knead until smooth and fairly soft. Roll out and use it to line a large shallow ovenproof dish. Bake blind (see Tip) for 15 minutes, or until the pie case is light golden brown.

4. Meanwhile, continue with the béchamel sauce. Strain the infused milk and set aside. Melt the butter for the sauce in the pot, stir in the flour, and cook over a gentle heat for 1 minute. Remove from the heat and gradually beat in the infused milk, a little at a time, until evenly blended. Return to a low heat and stir constantly until the sauce thickens. Bring to a gentle boil, still stirring, and simmer for about 2 minutes, then remove from the heat and set aside to cool.

5. To make the filling, cook the diced mixed vegetables in a saucepan of lightly salted boiling water until just tender. Drain and leave to cool. Heat a little butter in a small skillet and fry the mushrooms lightly, then remove and leave to cool. Add the onions to the skillet and fry lightly, then leave to cool.

6. Stir all the cooked vegetables into the béchamel sauce and season to taste.

7. Remove the pastry case from the oven, allow to cool a little, then remove the lining paper and fill with the vegetable mixture, spreading with a palette knife so that it is smooth and flat. Sprinkle with the Cheddar. Brush the edges of the pastry with the beaten egg yolk and return to the oven for 15 minutes, or until the cheese has melted and is beginning to brown. Serve hot.

TIP Baking blind means precooking a pastry base without a filling. After lining the dish with the pastry, prick it all over with a fork. Cut a piece of wax paper to the shape of the dish and about 2 inches larger all around, and place it over the pastry. Pour enough dried beans over the paper to cover it, then place in the oven for 15 minutes, as directed.

Serves 4 / Preparation time: 20 minutes / Cooking time: 25 minutes

Grilled Sausages with Mustard Mashed Potatoes

8 speciality sausages

2 onions, cut into wedges, roots left intact

Mustard mashed potatoes:

2 lb potatoes, scrubbed and quartered

6 tablespoons butter

1 tablespoon wholegrain mustard

3 teaspoons prepared English mustard

1 garlic clove, crushed

1 large bunch of parsley, chopped

dash of olive oil

salt and pepper

1. First make the mustard mashed potatoes. Cook the potatoes in a large saucepan of boiling water for about 20 minutes, or until tender.

2. Place the sausages on a preheated ridged grill pan and cook for 10 minutes, turning them to get an even color. Add the onion wedges and cook with the sausages for 6–7 minutes.

3. Meanwhile, drain the cooked potatoes well and return them to the pot. Place over a low heat and allow any excess water to steam away without coloring the potatoes. Remove from the heat, then, holding the warm potatoes in a dish towel, peel them carefully and mash well, using a potato masher or fork. Add the butter, wholegrain and English mustards, garlic, and salt and pepper, and continue to mash. Taste the potato and add more mustard, if liked. Finally, stir in the parsley and a dash of olive oil.

4. Serve the mashed potatoes and sausages together with the onion wedges.

Lamb Shanks with Olives and Sun-dried Tomatoes with Creamy Saffron Mashed Potatoes

2 tablespoons all-purpose flour

4 lamb shanks, about 1 lb each

2 tablespoons olive oil

2 red onions, sliced

2 tablespoons rosemary leaves

3 garlic cloves, chopped

½ cup balsamic vinegar

1 cup red wine

⅓ cup pitted black olives, quartered

⅓ cup sun-dried tomatoes, cut into strips lengthwise

¾ cup water

salt and pepper

Creamy saffron mashed potatoes:

2 lb potatoes, peeled and cut into large chunks

½ cup light cream

large pinch of saffron threads

5 tablespoons extra virgin olive oil

salt and pepper

1. Season the flour with a little salt and pepper, then toss the lamb in the flour, shaking off any excess.

2. Heat the oil in a flameproof casserole large enough to accommodate the lamb shanks in one layer. Add the lamb and brown well all over. Remove with a slotted spoon and set aside.

3. Lower the heat, add the onions, and cook for about 10 minutes, until softened. Add the rosemary and garlic and cook for a further 2–3 minutes. Increase the heat, add the balsamic vinegar and red wine, and boil rapidly until reduced by half. Stir in the olives, sun-dried tomatoes, and water.

4. Lower the heat again and place the lamb shanks on top of the sauce, cover with a tight-fitting lid, and cook for 1½–2 hours until very tender. Alternatively, cook in a preheated oven at 400°F. Check occasionally, basting the lamb shanks and adding more water if necessary.

5. Meanwhile, to make the saffron mashed potatoes, cook the potatoes in a large saucepan of boiling water for about 20 minutes, until just tender. Heat the light cream to simmering point in a small saucepan, remove from the heat, and stir in the saffron threads. Leave to infuse for 10 minutes.

6. When the potatoes are cooked, drain well, return to the dry pot, and add the saffron cream and oil. Mash together well using a potato masher or fork and season with salt and pepper to taste.

7. To serve, place a spoonful of the saffron mashed potatoes on each plate, top with a lamb shank, and spoon some sauce over the top.

4 x 1 lb Rock Cornish hens, chargrilled
(see page 20)

¼ cup sunflower oil

¼ cup shredded shallots

2 garlic cloves, crushed

⅓ cup shredded carrot

1 cup red lentils

1 cup chicken stock

4 teaspoons Thai red curry paste

1¾ cups diced sweet potatoes

1 teaspoon cumin seeds

small handful of cilantro, chopped

salt and pepper

Marinade:

¼ cup Dijon mustard

6 garlic cloves, crushed

½ cup sunflower oil

few sprigs of rosemary

To garnish:

olive oil, for drizzling

1 lemon, quartered

sprigs of rosemary

Chargrilled Rock Cornish Hens with Sweet Potatoes

1. To make the marinade, put the mustard and garlic into a blender or food processor. Blend the ingredients together, then, with the motor running, slowly pour in the sunflower oil to form a smooth paste. Transfer the paste to a large shallow dish and add the rosemary.

2. Turn the spatchcocked birds in the mustard mixture and coat them well. Cover and leave to marinate in the refrigerator for 24 hours.

3. Heat half of the oil in a large saucepan, add the shallots, garlic, carrot, and lentils, and turn in the oil. Add half the stock and bring to a boil. Lower the heat and simmer gently, adding more stock a ladleful at a time until all the stock has been used and the lentils are cooked. Stir in the curry paste and season with salt and pepper to taste. Cover and set aside.

4. Heat the remaining oil in another saucepan, add the sweet potatoes and cumin seeds, and fry for 7–10 minutes, until the sweet potatoes are soft but not colored.

5. Remove the hens from the marinade and cook under a preheated hot broiler or on a barbecue for 10 minutes on each side, or until tender and cooked through.

6. Meanwhile, gently reheat the lentil mixture and stir in the sweet potatoes and coriander. To serve, divide the lentil and sweet potato mixture between 4 warmed plates. Place the Rock Cornish hens on top and drizzle with a little olive oil. Garnish with the lemon quarters and sprigs of rosemary and serve hot.

Massaman Potato Curry

3¼ cups coconut milk

13 oz potatoes, cut into even-sized pieces

½ cup crushed roasted peanuts

1 large onion, chopped

5 tablespoons tamarind water

½ cup soft brown sugar

2 teaspoons salt

basil leaves, to garnish

Massaman curry paste:

3 cardamom pods

1 teaspoon coriander seeds

1 teaspoon cumin seeds

2 cloves

6 small fresh red chiles

2 garlic cloves, halved

1 teaspoon ground cinnamon

½ inch piece of fresh ginger root, peeled and finely chopped

3 shallots, chopped

1 lemon grass stalk, chopped

juice of ½ lime

To serve:

naan bread or rice

salad

1. First make the curry paste. Remove the seeds from the cardamom pods and dry-fry the cardamom seeds in a small skillet for 2 minutes with the coriander and cumin seeds and the cloves. Transfer the dry-fried spices to a blender or food processor and blend with the remaining curry paste ingredients to make a thick paste. Alternatively, use a pestle and mortar.

2. To make the curry, heat the coconut milk in a large saucepan and add 2 tablespoons of the curry paste or to taste. Stir to blend, then heat until simmering. (Transfer any remaining curry paste to an airtight container and store in the refrigerator for up to 3 weeks.)

3. Lower the heat, add the potatoes to the pot, and cook for 6 minutes.

4. Add the crushed roasted peanuts, onion, tamarind water, sugar, and salt. Stir thoroughly to dissolve the sugar and continue to simmer, stirring, for 5 minutes.

5. Increase the heat and allow the liquid to bubble until the potato is tender. Garnish with basil leaves before serving with naan bread or rice and a salad.

Serves 4 / Preparation time: 30–35 minutes, plus chilling / Cooking time: 25 minutes

Salmon Fish Cakes

10 oz potatoes, scrubbed

2 tablespoons butter or margarine

10 oz fresh salmon, cooked and flaked

2 tablespoons chopped parsley

2 eggs, beaten

½ cup dry natural bread crumbs

flour, for dusting

oil, for shallow-frying

salt and pepper

chives, to garnish

tomato salad, to serve

1. Cook the potatoes in a large saucepan of boiling water for about 20 minutes, or until tender. Drain well, then, holding the warm potatoes in a dish towel, peel them carefully.
2. Using a potato masher or fork, mash the potatoes in a bowl with the butter or margarine, then mix in the flaked salmon, parsley, salt and pepper to taste, and half of the beaten egg. Cover and chill for 20 minutes.
3. Place the salmon and potato mixture on a lightly floured surface and shape into a roll. Cut into 8 slices and shape each one into a flat round, about 2½ inches in diameter. Dip the rounds into the remaining beaten egg, then coat with bread crumbs.
4. Heat the oil in a skillet, add the fish cakes, in batches, and fry for 2–3 minutes on each side, or until golden brown and heated through. Garnish with chives and serve with a tomato salad.

**Serves 4–6 / Preparation time: 25 minutes / Cooking time: 1½–2 hours /
Oven temperature: 300–325°F**

Venison Stew with Parsnip and Potato Champ

1–2 tablespoons oil

1 onion, finely chopped

1½–2 lb lean, boneless venison, cut into
   1-inch cubes

¼ cup all-purpose flour

1¼ cups Guinness stout

3¼ cups game stock or water

1 bay leaf

1 sprig of marjoram

12–18 pearl onions, peeled

2–3 celery stalks, cut into 1-inch lengths

2 tablespoons finely chopped parsley

salt and pepper

Parsnip and potato champ:

1–1½ lb potatoes, peeled and cut into even-sized
   pieces

1–1½ lb parsnips, peeled and cut into even-sized
   pieces

butter, for mashing

salt and pepper

1. Heat half the oil in a large skillet and fry the onion until soft and beginning to brown. Transfer the onion to a large flameproof casserole.

2. Heat the remaining oil in the skillet and fry the meat, a little at a time, until brown. Add to the onion. Stir in the flour and add the Guinness stout, stock, bay leaf, and marjoram, and season with salt and pepper.

3. Bring to a boil, then lower the heat and simmer gently for 1–1½ hours until the meat is almost tender. (Alternatively, cook the stew in the oven at 300–325°F for the same length of time.) Add the pearl onions and celery about 20 minutes before the end of the cooking time.

4. Start making the parsnip and potato champ about 30 minutes before the stew will be ready. Cook the potatoes and parsnips separately in large saucepans of boiling water for about 20 minutes, or until tender. Drain and dry well, then mash together with plenty of butter and salt and pepper to taste, using a potato masher or fork.

5. To serve, taste the stew and adjust the seasoning if necessary. Stir in the parsley and serve with the parsnip and potato champ.

Serves 4 / Preparation time: 20 minutes / Cooking time: 40–45 minutes / Oven temperature: 400°F

Potato Tart with Ham, Artichokes, and Mushrooms

Potato dough:

6 tablespoons butter, plus extra, for greasing

1 onion, thinly sliced

1¼ cups all-purpose flour

½ cup cold, cooked mashed potato

salt and pepper

Topping:

1 tablespoon olive oil

2 shallots, sliced

2 cups mushrooms, sliced

4 oz cooked ham, cut into strips

1 cup drained canned artichoke hearts, sliced

salt and pepper

This free-form tart has a moist, biscuit-like dough, which is perfect for all sorts of savory toppings.

1. To make the dough, melt 2 tablespoons of the butter in a small saucepan. Add the onion and fry for about 5 minutes, until softened and lightly browned. Cool slightly.

2. Place the flour in a mixing bowl. Dice the remaining butter and rub it into the flour. Add the onion with the pan juices, the mashed potato, and salt and pepper, to taste. Mix to a soft dough. Preheat the oven to 400°F.

3. Press out the dough on a greased baking sheet to a 9-inch round. Pinch the edges of the dough upwards to make a slight rim.

4. To make the topping, heat the oil in a skillet, add the shallots, and fry until lightly browned. Add the mushrooms and cook briefly, until softened.

5. Scatter the ham and artichoke hearts over the dough, then top with the shallot and mushroom mixture. Season with salt and pepper and bake for 25–30 minutes, until the base is golden brown. Serve hot.

FOOD FACT The globe artichoke is the flower head of a type of thistle, probably native to North Africa but now cultivated in Europe and North America. Some of the artichoke's flavor lies in the fat base of each of its leaves, but the best part is its tender base, or heart, deep within the center of the vegetable. Artichoke hearts are available bottled in oil, canned, or frozen.

**Serves 6 / Preparation time: 40 minutes / Cooking time: 1¾ hours /
Oven temperature: 375°F**

Chicken and Mushroom Pie

3 lb chicken with giblets

1 bouquet garni

1 small onion, quartered

6–8 black peppercorns

2 tablespoons butter

2 leeks, trimmed, cleaned, and thinly sliced

2 cups sliced button mushrooms

1 teaspoon all-purpose flour

½ cup full-fat soft cheese

2 tablespoons chopped parsley

salt

sprigs of parsley, to garnish

Topping:

1 lb potatoes, peeled and cut into even-sized
  pieces

8 oz carrots, sliced

2 tablespoons butter

1 egg, beaten

pinch of ground nutmeg

salt and pepper

1. Put the chicken and giblets into a large saucepan with the bouquet garni, onion, black peppercorns, and a little salt. Cover with water, bring to a boil, then skim the surface. Cover the pot and simmer for about 1 hour, or until the chicken is cooked. To test, pierce the thickest part of the leg with a fine skewer—the juices should run clear.

2. Remove the chicken and set aside. When it is cool enough to handle, skin it and cut the meat from the bones. Place the chicken meat in an ovenproof dish and set aside. (Reserve the chicken stock for use in another recipe or for making soup.)

3. Melt the butter in a small skillet and fry the leeks and mushrooms over a moderate heat for 3 minutes, stirring. Stir in the flour, then the soft cheese and parsley. Simmer for 3 minutes, then spread the vegetables over the pieces of chicken.

4. To make the topping, cook the potatoes and carrots separately in large saucepans of lightly salted boiling water for about 20 minutes, or until tender. Drain well, then mash them together using a potato masher or fork, and beat in the butter and egg. Season to taste with nutmeg, salt, and pepper.

5. Preheat the oven to 375°F. Spread the potato and carrot topping evenly over the chicken and vegetables, then fork it up into peaks.

6. Bake for 20–25 minutes, until the topping is well browned. Garnish with sprigs of parsley and serve hot.

Serves 4 / Preparation time: 20 minutes, plus chilling / Cooking time: 20–25 minutes

Crab Cakes

¼ cup butter or margarine

1 onion, finely chopped

1 cup chopped mushrooms

½ cup all-purpose flour

⅔ cup milk

1 teaspoon Worcestershire sauce

2 tablespoons chopped parsley

1 cup fresh, canned, or frozen cooked crabmeat

8 oz cooked baking potatoes, mashed without
   any additional liquid

2 eggs, beaten

½ cup dry natural bread crumbs

¼ cup sunflower oil or butter

salt and pepper

1. Heat the butter or margarine in a saucepan. Add the onion and mushrooms and cook gently until soft. Add half of the flour and stir over a low heat for 2–3 minutes.

2. Blend in the milk and stir as the liquid comes to a boil and thickens. Season lightly with salt and pepper and add the Worcestershire sauce, parsley, and crabmeat.

3. Blend the mashed potatoes with the crabmeat mixture. Chill until firm enough to form into 8 round cakes.

4. Season the remaining flour and use to coat the crab cakes all over. Brush them with beaten egg, then roll in the dry bread crumbs.

5. Heat the sunflower oil or butter in a large skillet and cook the crab cakes, in batches, until crisp and brown on both sides.

Baked Cod with Potatoes and Olives

12 oz potatoes, thinly sliced

sprig of thyme, separated into leaves

4 cod fillets, about 7 oz each

2 tablespoons pitted black olives

2 tablespoons olive oil

butter, for greasing

salt and pepper

1. Preheat the oven to 425°F. Arrange the potatoes in layers in a well-buttered shallow ovenproof dish, sprinkling each layer with a little thyme, salt, and pepper.
2. Place the pieces of cod on top of the potatoes, add the olives, and drizzle with olive oil. Season with salt and pepper and add a little more thyme.
3. Place the dish in the middle of the oven and cook for 25 minutes. Check that the potatoes are soft before serving.

Sweet Potato and Spinach Curry

1. Cook the sweet potato chunks in a large saucepan of lightly salted boiling water for 8–10 minutes, or until tender. Drain well and set aside.
2. Heat the oil in a saucepan, add the onion, garlic, shrimp paste, and turmeric, and fry over a gentle heat, stirring frequently, for 3 minutes. Stir in the chile and fry for a further 2 minutes.
3. Add the coconut milk, stir to mix, then simmer for 3–4 minutes until the coconut milk has thickened slightly. Stir in the cooked sweet potatoes and some salt to taste, then cook the curry for 4 minutes.
4. Stir in the spinach, cover the pot, and simmer gently for 2–3 minutes, or until the spinach has wilted and the curry has heated through. Taste, and adjust the seasoning if necessary, then serve the curry immediately with naan bread, if liked.

1 lb sweet potatoes, peeled and cut into large chunks

3 tablespoons peanut oil

1 red onion, chopped

2 garlic cloves, crushed

1 teaspoon shrimp paste

1 teaspoon ground turmeric

1 large fresh red chile, seeded and chopped

1¾ cups coconut milk

8 oz ready-washed young leaf spinach

salt

naan bread, to serve (optional)

FOOD FACT Spinach is one of the most widely grown and popular of the leafy vegetables. It has a subtle, faintly bittersweet taste and its leaves may be small and rounded or larger and more pointed, curly or smooth. Spinach needs thorough washing to remove the grit often found within it. It is at its best eaten raw in salads or only lightly cooked, since it reduces greatly in volume when cooked. Spinach contains both iron and calcium, but the absorption of these minerals by the human body is inhibited by the oxalic acid also found in spinach.

**Serves 4 / Preparation time: 30 minutes, plus rising / Cooking time: 25 minutes /
Oven temperature: 475°F**

Potato Dough Calzone

Potato dough:

1½ cakes fresh yeast

1½ cups lukewarm water

3¼ cups strong all-purpose flour, plus extra for
working the dough

1 teaspoon salt

heaping ½ cup cooked and riced or sieved potato

butter, for greasing

Filling:

¾ cup cubed lean cooked ham

1½ cups cubed mozzarella cheese

1 cup ricotta cheese

1 teaspoon chopped basil

2 eggs, beaten, plus extra for glazing

salt and pepper

1. Begin by making the dough. Blend the yeast with a little of the lukewarm water. Sift the flour and salt into a large mixing bowl. Stir in the potato. Make a well in the center and pour in the yeast mixture and the remaining lukewarm water. Using your hand, and with a circular movement, gradually work the floury potato mixture into the liquid, working from the center of the well outwards to make a sticky, elastic dough.

2. Turn the dough onto a lightly floured surface and knead it well, adding more flour if necessary, until it is less sticky. Knead well for about 10 minutes until the dough becomes smooth and elastic.

3. Sprinkle the base of the mixing bowl with flour. Return the dough to the bowl, cover with a cloth, and leave the dough to rise until doubled in size—about 1 hour.

4. Meanwhile, mix all the filling ingredients together, adding salt and pepper to taste.

5. When the dough has risen, turn it onto a floured surface and divide into 8 pieces. Press each one out into a round about 6 inches in diameter. Preheat the oven to 475°F.

6. Divide the filling between the 8 rounds of dough. Moisten the edges of the rounds with a little water and fold each one over to form a semicircle, pinching the edges together well to seal them.

7. Brush the calzone with a little beaten egg. Place on a greased baking sheet and bake at the top of the oven for about 25 minutes, until well risen and golden brown.

FOOD FACT Calzone are small pizza turnovers. The ones in this recipe can be fried instead of baked. Fried calzone are softer and lighter than the baked variety, as they do not form a crust. To fry calzone, omit the egg glazing and fry them in hot, deep oil for about 4–5 minutes on each side. Drain well on paper towels and serve immediately.

Spanish Tortilla

This is an authentic Spanish omelet, which is traditionally made with just eggs, potatoes, onions, and salt and pepper, and cooked in a large amount of olive oil. This version contains sliced red and green bell peppers for extra color and flavor.

⅔ cup extra virgin olive oil

1½ lb potatoes, thinly sliced

1 large onion, sliced

1 red bell pepper, seeded and sliced

1 green bell pepper, seeded and sliced

5 large eggs, beaten

salt and pepper

salad, to serve (optional)

1. Heat all but 2 tablespoons of the oil in an 8-inch nonstick skillet. Add the potato slices, onion, and red and green peppers, and cook, stirring frequently, for 15 minutes, until all the vegetables are golden and tender.

2. Stir the potato mixture into a bowl containing the beaten eggs and season generously with salt and pepper. Set aside for 15 minutes. Clean the skillet.

3. Heat the remaining oil in the clean skillet and tip in the tortilla mixture. Cook over a low heat for 10 minutes until almost cooked through. Carefully slide the tortilla onto a large plate. Invert another plate over the tortilla and turn the plates upside down so that you can slide the tortilla back into the skillet, cooked side uppermost.

4. Return the pan to the heat and cook for a further 5 minutes, or until the tortilla is cooked on both sides. Allow to cool, then serve the tortilla at room temperature, cut into wedges and accompanied by a salad, if liked.

Malaysian Beef and Potato Curry

2 tablespoons peanut oil

5 shallots, chopped

2 garlic cloves, crushed

2-inch piece of fresh ginger root, grated

2 tablespoons hot curry powder

1 teaspoon ground cinnamon

1 teaspoon ground cumin

1 teaspoon ground coriander

¼ teaspoon ground cardamom

4 curry leaves

1 star anise

4 cloves

12 oz sirloin steak, cut into ½-inch strips

10 oz potatoes, peeled and cut into medium-
   sized chunks

2 large fresh red chiles, seeded and finely
   chopped

½ teaspoon salt

1¼ cups coconut milk

juice of 1 lime

1 teaspoon soft brown sugar

plain boiled rice, to serve

1. Heat the oil in a saucepan, add the shallots, garlic, and ginger, and fry over a gentle heat, stirring frequently, for 5 minutes, or until softened. Add the curry powder, ground cinnamon, cumin, coriander, cardamom, curry leaves, star anise, and cloves, and fry for a further 1 minute.

2. Add the strips of beef and stir well to coat in the spice mixture. Add the potatoes, chiles, salt, and coconut milk. Stir well to combine, bring to a boil, then lower the heat, cover the pot, and simmer gently, stirring occasionally, for 40 minutes, until the beef is tender and the potatoes are cooked.

3. Stir in the lime juice and sugar and cook, uncovered, for a further 2 minutes. Taste, adjust the seasoning, if necessary, then serve the curry hot, with plain rice.

Index